Praise for
Stop Moaning, Start Owning

"Baby boomers, Generation Xers, Generation Yers, Millennials—have I forgotten anyone?—wake up! The problem isn't them—it is you. In this book, Dr. Brian Russell explains why life is what you make it, not what you can get others to provide you. You are entitled to nothing. This book is like a condensed and cost-effective therapy session. Read it. Heed it. Find your contentment."

—**Diane Dimond**,
journalist, author, and syndicated columnist

"I recommend this book for both lawyers and nonlawyers. As an attorney and father of three, I believe this book will stimulate discussion concerning entitlement versus personal responsibility."

—**Mark Eiglarsh**,
national TV personality and attorney

"Read this important new book, give copies to all your kids and anyone else who wants to read about what needs fixing in the U.S.A."

—**Eric Tyson**,
bestselling author of
Personal Finance for Dummies

"Brian Russell has an incredible amount of experience when it comes to problem solving. His book wonderfully highlights the importance of taking personal responsibility in order to lead a more productive and successful life."

—**Stacy Kaiser**,
psychotherapist, author, and co-host of
Fatal Vows on Investigation Discovery

STOP MOANING, START OWNING

How Entitlement Is Ruining America and How Personal Responsibility Can Fix It

BRIAN RUSSELL, PhD, JD

Co-Host of the Series *Fatal Vows* on Investigation Discovery

Health Communications, Inc.
Deerfield Beach, Florida

www.hcibooks.com

Library of Congress Cataloging-in-Publication Data
is available through the Library of Congress

© 2015 Brian Russell

ISBN-13: 978-07573-1876-4 (Paperback)
ISBN-10: 07573-1876-2 (Paperback)
ISBN-13: 978-07573-1877-1 (ePub)
ISBN-10: 07573-1877-0 (ePub)

Publisher: Health Communications, Inc.
　　　　　3201 S.W. 15th Street
　　　　　Deerfield Beach, FL 33442–8190

Cover and interior design by Lawna Patterson Oldfield

Contents

Acknowledgments

Thanks to my parents, Kathleen and Timothy Russell, for instilling personal responsibility in me; to Dr. Richard Garland, for mentoring me as a psychologist; to radio's Dr. Laura Schlessinger, for inspiring me to make a difference on a national scale; and to TV's Bill O'Reilly for showing me how to argue my case before a national audience.

Additional thanks to my agent, Claudia Menza, agent/publicist Annie Scranton, and editor Christine Belleris for believing in this book and for all of their assistance in bringing it to you.

Introduction

In my years as cohost of the series *Fatal Vows* on Investigation Discovery, I've spotlighted people at their worst, those who've traveled far down profoundly destructive paths of their own choosing. As my colleague Dr. Drew Pinsky likes to remind me whenever I appear on his show, the cartoon series *South Park* has dubbed shows like mine "informative murder porn," implying that they don't have any value beyond voyeurism and Schadenfreude. I really don't think that's true, though. I always argue that many important lessons for everyday life, marriage, parenting, personal safety, and so on can be drawn from extreme cases with spectacularly bad endings. Perhaps chief among these lessons is how most bad endings—spectacular or not—could be prevented if only the people involved had made better choices earlier about their own behavior and about behavior they've tolerated from others.

In recent years, there's been an awful lot of moaning from an awful lot of unhappy Americans accompanied by an awful lot of excuses as to why *they're* not responsible for their unhappiness, economic circumstances, or behavior. You may have heard people make excuses for themselves, or maybe you've even said some of these things yourself. I'm embarrassed to say, many of these have been served up on silver platters by some of my fellow psychologists and lawyers:

- "I haven't succeeded because I've been oppressed by [a demographic group, corporate America, the rich]."
- "I've abused [my spouse, my kids, both] because I had a bad childhood."
- "I'm [obese, failing school, addicted] because I have a disease."
- "I was prevented from knowing right from wrong by [a mental illness, violent video games, too many Twinkies]."

These are just a handful of examples. An exhaustive list—from felons, philanderers, and freeloaders to everyday Americans with everyday gripes and everything in between—could fill this entire book. In short, America has become a nation with far too many narcissistic, self-entitled, excuse-making moaners who simply refuse to *own* their problems and the solutions thereto. But it wasn't always that way.

The United States was founded and built by rugged individualists, people who supremely valued personal freedom—the freedom to develop their ideas, strengths, skills, and talents to the best of their abilities in the pursuit of better lives for themselves, their families, and future generations. They were willing to take profound risks, like leaving their home continents for distant and unknown shores, like standing up to and defeating the most formidable foes of their times—more than once (e.g., Great Britain, Spain, Nazi Germany . . .)—and they literally tore their nation apart and pulled it back together again to eradicate the scourge of slavery.

They did all that in the name of freedom. And in their unrelenting quest for freedom—not just political and economic freedom, but also freedom of religion, expression, and association—they were successful beyond the founders' wildest imaginations. In the blink of an eye in the grand timeline of human history, they created a nation that surpassed all others in its industrial, cultural, and intellectual productivity; in its prosperity and peacekeeping power; and, yes, in its personal freedom, making it the single greatest nation in human history in which to pursue happiness.

The people who founded and built America understood that that's all their precious freedom meant—freedom to *pursue* happiness—and that none among them was guaranteed or entitled to actually *capture* it. They also understood that freedom and personal anarchy weren't the same, and that maximum personal freedom required reasonable limits so that each citizen's exercise of freedom wouldn't impinge or infringe upon the freedoms of others. Furthermore, they understood that such reasonable limits were best *self*-imposed, that it would be both impractical and oppressive to have a society in which behavioral limits were forced upon individuals by the state. In other words, they understood that personal freedom and personal responsibility went hand in hand.

I think they also tended to gauge happiness differently than many Americans do today. Think about the unemployed and underemployed professionals who went to work in coal mines to feed their families during the Great Depression. Think about our "Greatest Generation" of Americans who banded together and sacrificed profoundly to preserve not just their own freedom but also the freedom of others in distant lands during World War II. In contrast to many of today's Americans, I think they tended to gauge happiness in relation to their contributions to things larger than themselves—most centrally to their families, then rippling outward to their churches, professions, businesses, communities, country, and even their world.

But the further the nation has progressed beyond the early struggles that paved the way to its prosperity, the easier it has become for its people to perceive their "fair shares" of its prosperity less as privileges and more as entitlements. As successful as America became in an age of personal responsibility, over my professional lifetime I've seen it drifting with increasing inertia toward an age of entitlement. I've seen it in my personal life. I've seen it as I've assessed and counseled adults, adolescents, couples, and families as a psychologist. I've seen it as I've served as an expert witness in legal cases where parties' states of mind have been pivotal. I've seen it as I've negotiated and mediated disputes and represented clients in civil and criminal court as a lawyer. I've seen it as I've taught courses to undergraduate students and given lectures to groups of accomplished professionals from all over the country. I've seen it as I've run my own businesses and advised leaders of businesses large and small on how to solve productivity problems. I've seen it as I've advised legislators on how to draft laws to rein in various types of destructive behavior. I've seen it as I've analyzed virtually every major crime story that has made national news for the better part of a decade. And I've seen it as I've traveled the world comparing what's happening elsewhere to what's happening in America.

You've seen it, too. You've seen it in the skyrocketing rates of parental abandonment, divorce, and remarriage—three and four different last names living in the same single-family dwelling—and in the damage that does to the children involved, both while they're children and later, when they attempt to form healthy, enduring relationships and families of their own. You've seen it in the pervasive excuse-making by criminals who consciously choose to behave in heinously destructive ways and then, when caught, attribute their behavior to bad parenting, historical oppression, some compulsive behavioral "disease" like addiction (to drugs or sex), or psychosis. You've seen it in the escalating, unsustainable debt that Americans are carrying, both individually and collectively. You've seen it in the increasing numbers of claims for disability and other forms of public assistance when, in fact, the number of adult Americans who are mentally or physically incapable of sustaining themselves and their children are, thankfully, relatively small. You've seen it in the ever-increasing acceptance of recreational drug use, of sexual promiscuity (even among middle-school-age kids), of obesity as yet another "disease," all of which are driven by hedonistic impulses over which people are no longer expected to exert much, if any, self-control. And in the rare event when a behavioral problem *is* identified as such, you've seen an ever-increasing preference for the quickest possible fix, such as ADHD diagnoses and psychotropic prescriptions for millions of academically challenged American kids, the vast majority of whom probably could benefit as much or more from some intensive behavioral shaping by involved parents.

And American culture increasingly facilitates such destructive trends. Even Americans who haven't participated in them directly have often participated *indirectly* by allowing personally irresponsible behaviors to become social norms. Americans today have grown to accept all kinds of behaviors that previous generations identified as destructive and therefore ostracized. In addition, all kinds of flimsy excuses and empty apologies without amends are now widely accepted, even for deliberately destructive behavior—for example, minimizations like, "I'm only human," and "I made a mistake." Also widely accepted in America these days are externalizations like, "If only my wife had paid more attention to me, I wouldn't have strayed," and deflections like, "Who among us is to judge?"

America's founders wisely understood that the law can do only so much to promote responsible behavior, since a free society's behavioral norms will be determined far more by what people are willing to accept than by what their government will ever effectively prohibit. But in cases where it once was more helpful, even the law has devolved to be relatively useless. For example, thanks to "no-fault" divorce in virtually every U.S. jurisdiction, the law will now do more to enforce a gym membership contract than a marriage contract, awarding damages to the gym when a member stops paying, while dividing marital assets 50/50 when one spouse abandons his or her family to take up with an affair partner. Meanwhile, the kids watch and learn as the law slaps celebrity scofflaws on their wrists time and time again, as it does thousands of lesser-known scofflaws all across America on a daily basis.

Another problem is that fewer parents are present today in American homes to talk with kids about the values that built the nation, and many who are present are nevertheless either too self-absorbed or too misguided to bother. On top of that, fewer and fewer Americans are regularly attending church services, where behavioral restraint and interpersonal obligation are staples. Meanwhile, in our public schools, fewer and fewer teachers seem

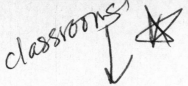

to desire or dare to go anywhere near an endorsement of traditional American values in the classroom for fear of being accused of moralizing and getting fired or sued. If a teenage student, for example, wrote a paper about how much she liked the reality TV series *16 and Pregnant*, what percentage of public school teachers do you think would actually say to the student, "No sixteen-year-old should be pregnant"?

It's really no wonder, then, that employers increasingly tell me about young Americans who, instead of appearing poised to out-perform their surging global competitors, appear self-entitled, disrespectfully assertive, lazy, interpersonally inept, even untrustworthy. And the American media generally doesn't help matters either. Virtually everywhere they go today, young (and old) Americans are bombarded by music, TV, movies, and advertising, all of which insidiously reinforce instant short-term gratification, often in the context of largely undeserved athletic and entertainment hero worship. And if Narcissus (the Greek mythological figure who fell in love with his reflection and the namesake of "narcissism") were alive today, social media no doubt would be his "reflecting pool" of choice.

All of these conditions reflect and facilitate a pervasive cultural shift away from personal responsibility and a similarly pervasive cultural shift toward *collective* responsibility for behavior, both of which are harming Americans and the country profoundly. In other words, Americans are accepting neither *accountability*, personal responsibility for behaving badly in the past (preferring to blame others, if anyone), nor are they accepting the *obligation*, the personal responsibility to behave well in the present and future (preferring their—ahem—"weight" to be pulled by others).

In short, despite how blessed Americans may be compared to the majority of people around them, let alone in their world, we're hearing an awful lot of moaning in America these days.

We're hearing a lot of moaning about how people aren't as happy as they think they deserve to be. Even many trained counselors, by remaining religiously value-neutral, implicitly give their patients license to pursue happiness regardless of the impact of their pursuit upon their spouses, children, and colleagues. We're also hearing a lot of moaning about how entitled people are to have both their needs and their *wants* met, often by others. It's good to be charitable when we're actually helping people who are in dire straits through no fault of their own, are doing everything they can for themselves, and are using our help appropriately, but when we're doing for others that which they could do for themselves, we're often enabling dysfunction rather than helping. And we're hearing a lot of moaning about how people's bad behavior isn't really their fault after all. In recent years, mass shootings in schools and workplaces have illustrated the extremes of entitlement, where an individual chooses to self-gratify or self-soothe at the expense of innocent others' very mortality. (I refer to that as "evil," or, if you prefer a more secular term, "psychopathy.") Yet even after consciously planning and concealing such evil over weeks and months, such shooters—the ones who stick around to see the aftermath of their evil instead of killing themselves to escape justice—routinely claim not to have known what they were doing or that it was wrong.

All of this moaning reflects an alarmingly increasing focus on the *self* when it comes to "rights" and an alarmingly increasing focus on *others* when it comes to obligations among Americans.

This approach to life is profoundly unproductive because even people with legitimate moans usually can change their own attitudes and behaviors far more easily than they can change the past, others, their workplaces, or society. Based on my years of comparative study and professional practice involving people (psychology), public policy (law), and productivity (business), I have come to believe that entitlement is the single most destructive common thread that binds most of America's social ills in this day and age. It causes people either to stagnate or to regress rather than to make any real progress in their lives, relationships, careers, and communities.

So is there a cure? Yes, I believe there is. We need a lot less moaning and a lot more "owning" both as individuals and as a nation. Wherever possible, we need to reassert *personal* responsibility for our problems and their solutions. Personal responsibility comes in two forms: accountability and obligation, both of which are profoundly important to a healthy, successful life. Personal responsibility has a downside as well as an upside. The downside is that it deprives people of excuses for unproductive behavior. In the therapy room, courtroom, classroom, boardroom, and on radio and television, I've heard just about every conceivable excuse in the book, and they're rarely valid. The upside of personal responsibility, though, is that it *empowers* and *motivates* individuals to take control of their destinies. After all, if you're not responsible for a past behavior, then how can you be expected to behave differently in the future?

At the same time, research both in positive psychology (the study of what's right with functional people rather than what's wrong with dysfunctional people) and in the emerging discipline of behavioral economics (the study of incentives and of what really motivates people to behave constructively vs. destructively) dovetails nicely with most major world religions to suggest that the acceptance of obligation to identify your unique abilities and to develop those abilities so that you contribute unique value to something larger than yourself generally maximizes your chances for material prosperity as well as personal fulfillment, especially when those rewards are surveyed through a lens of gratitude.

Despite having made a career of pointing out and prescribing fixes for Americans' individual and collective behavioral errors, I remain highly optimistic that if enough of us are motivated to do so, we can still swing our cultural pendulum back in the direction of personal responsibility, thereby achieving better, more productive lives individually and a better, more productive country collectively. This book is dedicated to that effort.

PART I:

STOP
MOANING!

CHAPTER 1

But I'm Not Happy!

> We hold these truths to be self-evident,
> that all men are created equal, that they are endowed
> by their Creator with certain unalienable Rights,
> that among these are Life, Liberty, and the
> *pursuit* [emphasis added] of Happiness.
>
> —Declaration of Independence, July 4, 1776

THE PURSUIT OF HAPPINESS

Happiness. We all want it. The right to pursue it is even enshrined in the United States' founding document. But what does "happiness" really mean? Is it good fortune, material prosperity? Merriam-Webster's online dictionary says that definition is obsolete. Is it hedonistic pleasure, freedom from

physiological pain, or, as the dictionary puts it, "a pleasurable
or satisfying experience"? Is it psychological comfort, a carefree
mind occupied only by positive thoughts and feelings, or, again
according to the dictionary, "a state of well-being and contentment"? For many of us, part of happiness is having our wants
as well as our needs fulfilled, but whose responsibility is it to
secure those for us? Most of us agree that guilt and shame are
unhappy feelings, often accompanied by unhappy consequences
in the aftermath of bad behavior. But if we've behaved badly,
then how should we feel, and what should our consequences be?

One evening in late September 2009, I appeared on a national
TV talk show to discuss legal issues surrounding the 2007 death
of Anna Nicole Smith, the former model who had married an
elderly billionaire and become a reality TV star before spiral-
ing into the oblivion of addiction. A caller to the show, Melody
from Ohio, asked whether Smith's doctors appeared to have done
enough to validate her need for the multiple prescriptions found
in her possession at the time of her death. In directing Melody's
question to me, Host Jane Velez-Mitchell noted that Smith's adult
son had died of a fatal prescription-drug overdose in the months
leading up to Smith's own fatal overdose. In my response, I stated
the following:

> We've become a quick-fix culture in which happiness is to be pur-
> sued by the fastest road, or what looks like the fastest road, as opposed
> to the most lasting or meaningful road. People don't want to do any-
> thing hard. They don't want to overcome any obstacles. But parts of
> life, like losing a loved one, *are* hard, and there's growth to be obtained
> by overcoming obstacles. . . .

I wish that people would start looking for their happiness not at the
bottom of a pill bottle or an alcohol bottle but by actually working
through these difficult issues and overcoming these obstacles.

Without a doubt, Smith's son's suicide was a profoundly trau-
matic event, the likes of which could send any parent into a dark
psychological place. But, like numerous celebrities, Smith had
immersed herself in a mind-numbing fog of prescription drugs
for years prior to that event. Whenever a celebrity attempts or
commits suicide, whether intentionally (e.g., Freddie Prinze,
Kurt Cobain, Robin Williams), or recklessly by mixing potentially lethal substances without sufficient concern as to whether
the result could be fatal (e.g., Whitney Houston), viewers and
readers invariably ask me how someone who apparently "has it
all"—youth, vitality, fame, money, sex appeal—can nevertheless be indifferent as to whether they live or die, especially in the
absence of some precipitating tragedy.

The answer, I believe, involves a misguided notion about the
pursuit of happiness. I've often heard celebrities describe their
overall goal or purpose in life as "to be happy," or something
along those lines, which they seem to define in terms of feeling
good, experiencing pleasure, escaping pain, and being comfortable and carefree in the present moment. Nineteen-seventies rock
star Sid Vicious said it multiple ways, such as, "I've only been in
love with a beer bottle and a mirror," "I just cash in on the fact
that I'm good looking, I've got a nice figure, and girls like me,"
and, "I'll die before I'm twenty-five, and when I do, I'll have lived
the way I wanted to."[1] Vicious was correct about at least one
thing—he died at twenty-one of a heroin overdose.

Personally, I don't believe that "to be happy" is really why each of us is here on Earth, and I don't think the pursuit of happiness as an end in and of itself actually gets anyone there. In a July 2014 *New York Times* article about happiness, author Arthur C. Brooks quotes tenth-century Moorish king Abd Al-Rahman III, who assumed his throne as a young man and enjoyed tangible abundance far beyond that of any modern-day American celebrity, reflecting upon his life:

> I have now reigned above fifty years in victory or peace; beloved by my subjects, dreaded by my enemies, and respected by my allies. Riches and honors, power and pleasure, have waited on my call, nor does any earthly blessing appear to have been wanting to my felicity. . . . I have diligently numbered the days of pure and genuine happiness which have fallen to my lot: They amount to fourteen.

Many modern-day celebrities who've attempted or committed suicide have a kindred spirit in Al-Rahman in that they've exhibited an incredulous despondency upon realizing that, despite acquiring all the tangible trappings of happiness, they've remained unhappy. Unfortunately, American celebrities who continue to spout the nonsense that one's purpose in life is "to be happy" are at the forefront of a hedonistic (and, ultimately, nihilistic) "if-it-*feels*-good-it-*is*-good" movement within America, which encourages instant gratification vs. delayed gratification, acting on feelings vs. thoughts, and the prioritization of the self vs. things larger than the self. Meanwhile, the converse of the "if-it-*feels*-good-it-*is*-good" mentality—"if-it-feels-*bad*-it-*is*-bad"—encourages the avoidance and eradication of all pain and negative feelings from people's lives. Thus, many Americans have equated happiness with the experience of pleasure and the absence of pain in the here and now.

I recently came across this social media post from a user with the Twitter handle "@psychologically": "Stop caring what people think. Stop taking caution in your actions, listen to what you want, do what you want, this is your life. Live it." The user's tagline read, "Follow us to know the science of the mind. Human Psychology, Social Behaviorism and Human Development." And at the time of that particular posting, over 300,000 people were in fact following @psychologically. Now, I don't know whether @psychologically actually has any legitimate credentials in psychology, behaviorism, or human development—anyone can claim to be anything on social media—but if the above tweet is representative of what they're promoting, then their sizable following is troubling to me, because the advice is not very productive.

FEELING GROOVY

Since Simon and Garfunkel first sang "The 59th Street Bridge Song"—or as most people know it, "Feeling Groovy"—to the nation back in 1966, Americans have placed a lot of cultural emphasis on feeling good, about themselves especially, beginning in childhood. While well-intentioned, that emphasis has served as the pretext for some profoundly un-American behavior. For example, in the summer of 2013, after a nine-year-old boy won a fifth-straight summer reading contest sponsored by his local library in Hudson Falls, New York, the library's director decided to end the boy's winning streak. Ostensibly out of concern that

repeatedly losing the contest would somehow damage or discourage kids who read less, the director decided to start awarding
prizes based on a random drawing rather than upon the number
of books read. And when an assistant librarian of twenty-eight
years stood up for the boy—who reportedly read over sixty books
in six weeks—and said that he deserved to claim the top prize,
she was *fired*![2]

Also in 2013, as the end of a semester approached, a Massa-
chusetts school principal made national news when he canceled
Honors Night, an event recognizing the academic achievements
of his school's best and brightest students, for fear that it might
harm the self-esteem of lesser-achieving students. What's more,
national reaction to the principal's decision was nowhere near
universally opposed. Many Americans readily endorsed the
notion that the lesser-achieving students' need for self-esteem
outweighed the higher-achieving students' need for recognition.

Then, in the spring of 2014, some of my colleagues with PhDs
got involved. Writing in an obscure academic publication titled
the *Journal of Experimental Education*,[3] they nevertheless made
national headlines with the thesis that the educational benefits
of homework were no longer worth the stress that it was causing
American kids. Having tutored dozens of K–12 students during my college and graduate school years, I was immediately
skeptical. Rarely did the kids I tutored have as much homework
as I had when I was their ages, and even more rarely did they
seem all that worried about it. In fact, far more often, I thought
they should've been *more* worried about it! Well, sure enough,
a Brookings Institute report on trends in American education
released that same year showed that it wasn't the homework that

had changed—American kids' homework loads had remained essentially constant since the 1980s[4]—it was our *culture* that had changed, as is evident in extracurricular contexts, too.

I didn't know whether to laugh, cry, or both when the Omaha (Nebraska) Public School Board president in 2013 faced fervent opposition after he proposed requiring students to maintain grade point averages of at least 2.0—a C average—in order to be eligible to play interscholastic sports. Opponents moaned that imposition of the requirement would disproportionately punish student athletes in certain demographic groups and harm their self-esteem when, in fact, increased motivation to maintain GPAs of (at least) 2.0 and increased time off of the playing field to spend on their studies when necessary would, in the long run, disproportionately *help* those very students and *raise* their self-esteem!

Meanwhile, you've undoubtedly heard about the lack of score-keeping and the distribution of participation trophies to everyone playing in sports programs for elementary-school-age kids across the country, so as not to harm the self-esteem of smaller and less-coordinated kids (of which I was one!), but you may be less aware of just how far that philosophy has permeated middle and high school sports. In 2013, a parent's complaint against a Texas high school football coach made headlines accusing the coach of "bullying" an opposing team's players? How, allegedly? By defeating them, 91–0. The coach of the winning team said he started substituting players in the first quarter and the game clock ran continuously starting in the second half, so he wasn't intentionally padding the score. Even the coach of the losing team said he disagreed with the parent who filed the bullying complaint. Still, the complaining parent told the media, "I did not know what to say on the ride home to explain the behavior of the [winning team's] coaches for not easing up when the game was in hand."[5]

How about just saying, "Gee, son, that was a tough one"? Maybe adding, "But at least there are always things to learn from playing really good teams like that." Wonder if that parent also thinks the United States should be "easing up" on its global military and economic competition. Frighteningly, I wouldn't be surprised.

And while it's bad enough that misguided adults are striving to prevent kids from experiencing self-esteem-threatening feelings of being bested in the classroom and on the athletic field, in other extracurricular contexts, similarly misguided adults are striving to prevent kids from experiencing self-esteem-threatening feelings of being excluded. How? By, for example, purging references to Christmas (a national holiday) from public school calendars, decorations, musical programs, and so on, and banning in-school observances of Halloween and Valentine's Day traditions, sparing kids exposure to the traditions of others in the name of inclusiveness. Doesn't sound very inclusive to me.

Being bested by others in the classroom or on the athletic field isn't being bullied; it's being challenged—to either improve or to find another pursuit to which one's better suited. Being benched until one's able to both learn and play a sport isn't being discriminated against; it's being protected—from frittering away the thing that's far more likely to determine one's future success in life, one's education, in favor of something that's more fun but fleeting. Merely being exposed to the beliefs of others isn't being oppressed; it's being culturally tolerant. In America, everyone has the right to go through life without being forced to embrace another's belief, but no one has the right to go through life without being exposed to, or even feeling offended by, another's belief. And when people make disingenuous allegations of bullying, discrimination, oppression, and so forth, they accomplish two reprehensible results: they malign the alleged perpetrators of those offenses unjustly, and they erect hurdles of skepticism that genuine victims of injustice must then overcome.

If it was just schoolchildren moaning about their need to feel good about themselves, we could chalk it up to mere immaturity, but *adults* are often the ones who are moaning! Several years ago, an article in the *Kansas City Star* began by lamenting how much "anxiety" soon-to-be college graduates were feeling, poised to enter an American job market softened by what had been dubbed the "Great Recession." Personally, I wasn't seeing it—hundreds of undergraduate students take my college course every spring, and they didn't seem particularly anxious to me. So, I read on, and what I saw was more arrogance than anxiety. One impending graduate moaned in the article about the scarcity of jobs that he'd feel "happy" doing. In his next breath, the young man moaned that *previous* generations of Americans "could pick and choose what they wanted to do." "I want to do that, too," he moaned, "but it's not the land of opportunity like it once was."[6] I was so alarmed at the thought of young Americans with attitudes like his competing head-to-head economically against some of the young Chinese with whom I've spoken when I've visited their country—hungry for opportunities to work hard and have things that previous generations of their families never had—that I titled my next column for WorldNetDaily "Bring On the Anxiety!"

In that column, I questioned how professionals—lawyers, doctors, bankers—who had gone to work in coal mines in order to
feed their families during a time when the threat to America's
economic viability *actually* warranted the "Great" modifier (the
Great Depression) would have reacted upon hearing a twenty-
two-year-old say that they had gotten to "pick and choose what
they wanted to do"! I noted that being happy in one's job is ideal,
and a worthy goal, but that it's a *luxury* that generally has to be
earned (and, even then, circumstances like bad economies, wars,
and personal crises can intervene) and that there's much to be
gained in terms of professional and character development in
the pursuit of that goal prior to its attainment. Yet, to quote the
headline of an August 19, 2013, Forbes.com article by Maura
Pennington, "Millions of millennials live at home and support
the policies that keep them there."

Notwithstanding, an analysis of the American Freshman Survey,[7] a questionnaire tracking the attitudes of college students
since the 1960s, has found that the percentages of respondents
who rate themselves as "above average" in various areas such
as writing ability, mathematical ability, and overall academic
ability have steadily risen. Over the same span of time, however,
the results of objective tests of writing ability, for example, have
trended in the opposite direction, suggesting that college students
in the 1960s actually tended to be stronger writers than today's
college students. Interestingly, a simultaneously declining measure has been students' self-reported time spent on their ever-so-
stressful homework.

LADIES AND GENTLEMEN, THE ESTEEMED . . . SELF

Americans, young and not so young, have thoroughly conflated the concepts of self-esteem and self-respect, between which distinction is critical. Merriam-Webster's online dictionary defines "self-respect" as "1) proper respect for oneself as a human being, or 2) regard for one's own standing or position." That same dictionary defines "self-esteem" as "1) a confidence and satisfaction in oneself: self-respect, or 2) self-conceit." If you just look at the first definition of "self-esteem," it appears synonymous with self-respect, but if you look closer, that second definition is something quite different. Unfortunately, that latter definition of "self-esteem"—"self-conceit"—better describes what I believe has been instilled in too many Americans.

As I see this distinction in practice, to "respect" oneself means according oneself, and expecting from others, recognition of one's inherent worth and basic human dignity and decent treatment. This is what the objective should have been, which should be unconditional. To "esteem" oneself, on the other hand, has come to mean according oneself, and expecting from others, recognition of one's unique worth and elevated status and the accompanying deferential treatment, as one might accord a brave soldier or police officer, a learned professor, a wise jurist, an eminent surgeon, or an artist or entertainer who has refined their gift of talent to near perfection—and which should be conditioned upon some worthy behavior.

Unfortunately, conflation of these two concepts has since adversely affected a couple of generations of Americans, many

of whom now tend to esteem themselves regardless of the quality of their behavior, and that's healthy neither for them nor for
the relationships, families, organizations, and communities in
which they're involved. One should not feel extra good about
(i.e., should not "esteem," in my view) oneself unless one's behavior has *been* extra good, and learning to cope with the unhappy
feelings of not having behaved in accordance with one's own or
with esteemed others' hopes or expectations is an important part
of one's healthy development. Sparing those unhappy feelings is
sparing maturation.

SELF-ESTEEM	SELF-RESPECT
Unique Worth	Inherent Worth
Elevated Status	Basic Dignity
Expectation of Deference	Expectation of Decency

We've probably all come across email forwards, tweets, Facebook posts, and so on, like the following, which I recently discovered online, attributed to "Salah Ali": "The ultimate goal in life is
to be happy without hurting anybody," and, "Think good about
yourself, love yourself, admire yourself, be happy with yourself,
smile, laugh, enjoy and live the beautiful life." Sound good? I like
the part about not hurting anybody, but when people think good
about themselves and love themselves and admire themselves
unconditionally, "unconditionally" tends to become "excessively," "excessively" tends to become "deservedly," "deservedly"
tends to become "at the expense of others," and the "without
hurting anybody" part tends to disappear.

As Americans have grown up internalizing expectations that they deserve to feel good and not to feel bad—in general, but particularly *about themselves*—it seems like many have psychologically twisted the right to the pursuit of happiness into the right to the *attainment* of happiness, which has been used to rationalize and justify a whole host of destructive behaviors such as substance abuse, promiscuity, marital infidelity, neglectful parenting, even crimes (up to and including mass murder), all of which generally lead—at least in the long run if not also in the short run—to isolation and despair rather than happiness.

MAKE ME HAPPY THIS INSTANT!

Like Anna Nicole Smith, many Americans have pursued happiness through the use and abuse of chemicals, legal and illegal. With respect to the former (legal substances), the pharmaceutical industry, as well as many of my colleagues in the healthcare professions, have been all too willing to promote and facilitate those misguided pursuits. The truth is that there's no chemical shortcut to happiness. At best, chemicals can only produce illusions of happiness that tend to fade away as quickly as the chemicals that produced them.

Meanwhile, many Americans have pursued happiness through the use and abuse of others, as if they have a right not just to the pursuit of happiness, and not even just to the attainment of happiness, but to the attainment of happiness at others' expense. For example, on the Investigation Discovery series *Fatal Vows*, which I've co-hosted since 2012, we've spotlighted an alarming shift in the way in which many Americans seem to be viewing marriage—as if the purpose of their marriages' and their spouses' very existence is to make *them* happy. During Season 3, one of my "fans" (although I doubt she's a fan anymore) may have spotlighted that attitude even better than we did on the show.

We aired an episode about an older couple whose marital death spiral began late in their marriage when they realized they weren't in agreement about how and where they wanted to spend their retirement years. Hours before that episode aired, I posted a link on Facebook and Twitter to an *AARP.org* article that explained some reasons why such conflicts increasingly cause long-married couples to divorce, and I added the following: "Differences re: #retirement plans = a growing cause of #divorce. Watch tonight's #FatalVows for more reasons why!" Shortly thereafter, the fan initiated the following sadly illustrative exchange on my Facebook page (with the fan's name and a couple of off-topic remarks omitted):

Fan: I think we are always growing & changing throughout life, & that doesn't always mean we're going in the same direction as our spouse / partner / friend / family member. . . . Even after, or maybe especially after, long periods of time. I believe that everyone deserves happiness. We all should know that that happiness is up to us alone. If I feel that I had grown to a point that I'd be happier elsewhere, then I would have to go. Even after long periods of time, time is too short to live unfulfilled.

Me: Sorry, but that kind of thinking is what's wrong with America. If one has mutually vowed to do certain things for life, then unless one's spouse has broken the vows first (in some material way, e.g., abuse, adultery, or addiction), one who breaks the vows simply because he or she isn't feeling "happy" keeping them at some point is not a person of character and integrity. That's a very selfish, entitled way to view a solemn commitment to another human being. I hope that any prospective spouse of one who thinks like that is aware that, to that person, vows apparently are just options, to be kept only unless/until something better comes along.

Fan: . . . I'm pretty sure that there's more wrong with this country than people who believe that it's better to end an unhappy relationship despite what they may have promised years beforehand than to continue unhappy & unhealthily through life. Being mature enough to go your separate ways instead of selfishly murdering the partner, or hiring someone else to "get rid" of the perceived unhappiness for you. That seems to me to be more of a problem with the world than anything I felt about the subject of long-term "vow" keeping. I'm in a long term committed relationship. If we ever decide to make it a legal affair there will be no vow of "forever." Do my best, & give my all, committed for a long time, yes, but "forever" is unrealistic to me, I won't "vow" it, & that doesn't mean that I'm, nor people who think as I do, a problem for America. . . .

Me: . . . If you choose to never make marriage vows, great. If you don't intend to stay with the person unless you're happy the whole time, then I'm glad to hear that at least you don't expect another human being to commit to you for life either. I wouldn't wish your attitude toward commitment on anyone, yourself included. You see, vows generally aren't as necessary when everything's good and everyone's "happy"; it's when not everything's good and not everyone's happy that vows come in to hold marriages together. You're also wrong when you suggest that spouses murdering one another is a bigger problem for America than people thinking as you do about marriage. Mariticide (the murder of one's spouse) is an extreme manifestation of narcissistic entitlement—divorcing one's spouse in the absence of a vows violation by the spouse is a less-extreme-but-more-common manifestation that's actually more damaging to more people in the aggregate. Statistically speaking, despite what

viewers around the world see on *Fatal Vows* every week, mariticide hardly
ever occurs, but people file for divorce all the time, not because their
spouses violated their marriage vows by abusing them or by betraying
them or by choosing drugs/alcohol over them, etc., but simply because
they're not "happy." The aggregate damage that's been inflicted upon
children in this country by that attitude toward the sanctity of marriage
vows is many, many, many times greater than the damage that's been
inflicted by mariticide. It's disgustingly emotionally abusive when the children of a marriage are minors, but it's still damaging even when they're
not. It's affected the ways in which entire generations of Americans view
not only marriage but commitments and obligations in life in general, and
not for the better. Thanks to the behavior of parents who think like you do,
more and more Americans are growing up to think like you do, and so the
cycle goes. Just as it wasn't good for them as children, it's not going to
be good for their children, it's not good for our culture/society (because it
leads to all kinds of personally irresponsible behavior from promiscuity to
academic and workplace productivity problems, to over-indebtedness to
crime . . .), and ironically, it's also highly unlikely to make them "happy"
as adults because it leads to weak attachments and superficial, underval-
ued, "throwaway" relationships. And you're wrong again to suggest that
people who've divorced their spouses simply because they haven't been
"happy" have had, as their alternatives, staying unhappy and unhealthy (as

if one must be "happy" to be healthy) for the rest of their lives or commit-
ting/soliciting their spouses' murders. No, a healthy and legal alternative
would've been to have stayed and worked on their marriages, like they
vowed to do. I'm currently writing a book about entitlement attitudes, the
devastatingly destructive behaviors that flow from them, and the need for
inherently good Americans to use their intellects more, their emotions less,
and recommit themselves to living personally responsible lives.

So, how does that fan's attitude work out in real life? Well, in 2015, *Titanic* actress Kate Winslet gave a profanity-laden interview to *Harper's Bazaar* in which she discussed having been married three times and having had three children, each with a different father. Winslet seemed to suggest that her need to feel good about herself was the paramount and prerequisite need in each of those relationships. She even went so far as to rationalize that her husband-hopping had actually been *good* for the three kids because . . . wait for it . . . it had taught them to *struggle*. "I think it's very important to teach your children to struggle on some level," she said, ". . . And I would honestly say, hand on heart, that I wouldn't change a thing. Even all the bad bits. Because it doesn't matter how crap times have been; they all matter for something—more than something, actually—because those are the things that shape who you are." Then came the interview's pièce de résistance: "And if you don't like who you are, well, then you're ******ed, really, aren't you?"[8]

FEELING GOOD VS. BEING GOOD

I see far too many everyday Americans—not the ones in Hollywood or on *Fatal Vows* or on the news—equating happiness with feeling good in the short run rather than being good in the long run, when in fact, the latter correlates with happiness far better. And regardless of what some of my psychobabbling colleagues may say in misguided efforts to help people like Ms. Winslet escape unpleasant guilt feelings, one's adult happiness is *not* a prerequisite to one's child's happiness. Witnessing the hell that many American parents put kids through in the name of adults' happiness (divorcing, remarrying, marginalizing existing kids by making new kids with new spouses, etc.) makes me want to wring those parents' necks.

Now, lest anyone dismiss Kate Winslet's experience as a one-off example of poor prioritization by someone who's a talented artist but perhaps not such a talented intellect, many otherwise-brilliant individuals have done tremendous damage to their families in the name of happiness. In July 2014, a Silicon Valley executive and married father of five turned up dead of a heroin overdose in the company of a paid female escort (who eventually pled guilty to the involuntary manslaughter of the executive). His sad story—or, more accurately, his kids' and wife's sad story—demonstrated how even highly intelligent individuals can use happiness to ratio-nalize profoundly selfish behavior, which usually ultimately leaves those individuals, and those for whom they're supposed to care, profoundly unhappy.

Neither sex outside of one's marriage nor substance abuse is *ever* a path to sustained happiness. Yet actions that actually might produce sustained happiness—like prioritizing the needs of your children over your wants, refocusing on your marriage, and cutting back or giving up distractions from your spousal and parental obligations—tend not to feel as good in the short run. Watch just about any American sitcom long enough, and there'll be a scene in which somebody says something like, "Of course it didn't feel good. The right thing never feels good. That's how you know it's the right thing!"

And as I've been discussing for years on the news and on *Fatal Vows*, the attitude that one is owed happiness, even at the expense of others, precipitates not only a lot of immoral behavior but also a lot of criminal behavior. For example, in December 2013 Harvard student Eldo Kim emailed a bomb threat to that university in order to evacuate campus buildings. Why? Because he didn't feel prepared to take a final exam scheduled for that day. When Kim was arrested, his lawyer nonchalantly explained away his behavior as the product of "pressure" (maybe Harvard assigned him too much homework), as if every college student doesn't feel some pressure around final exams and as if his client's actions didn't put pressure on everyone else on the campus that day—who, you may recall, lived, worked, and studied in the same community where a couple of homemade bombs had been detonated at the Boston Marathon just months prior, killing and injuring numerous innocent people.

Apparently, Kim didn't just feel pressure. Implicit in his actions also is a feeling that he was owed a reprieve from the pressure, by whatever means necessary. Not only that; he apparently felt that his was an exclusive right not to endure pressure because, in the process of escaping from pressure, he inflicted far more severe pressure upon thousands of innocent people. (So how did the American federal court system treat Kim? I'll tell you in Chapter 4.) And if you really think about it, virtually all of the school shootings that we've seen in recent years have been the products of similar attitudes, that the shooters were owed something—revenge for hurt feelings, a chance to feel in control for once in their pathetic lives, or some other form of self-soothing or self-gratification at the expense of others' very lives. We all feel insulted, disempowered, pressured, and so on at various times in our lives, but instead of resolving those feelings by behaving destructively toward others—especially toward others who had nothing to do with causing our hurt feelings—we can and must identify constructive ways to resolve them, and the responsibility to do so is solely our own.

MAKE ME HAPPY, AMERICA!

Then on a whole other level, many Americans today seem to feel that they have a right not just to the pursuit of happiness, not just to the attainment of happiness, not even just to the attainment of happiness at the expense of others, but to the attainment of happiness at the expense of the *entire society*! Yes, some misguided Americans actually believe that their right to happiness should be codified and made a goal of public policy. A November 2014 article in another obscure academic publication, *Policy Insights from the Behavioral and Brain Sciences*, argued that people's happiness, which the authors essentially equated with people's self-reported comfort, should be the standard by which we measure the success of our public policies. The third-world nation of Bhutan has been using that standard for decades—it even has a "Gross National Happiness Commission." Want to move there? I'll pass.

But U.S. House of Representatives Minority Leader Nancy Pelosi sounded like she would've liked to import Bhutan's policy to the United States when she said in 2014 that among the aims of providing taxpayer-subsidized health insurance to low-income Americans was to give them "liberty to pursue their happiness," which she went on to explain meant to "not be 'job-locked,' but to follow their passion."[9] Want to subsidize others' insurance in part so that they can leave their jobs and follow their passion? I'll pass again (nor do I want you to subsidize my insurance so that I can follow my passion, much as I'd like to see if I really might be able to take my tennis game to the pro level!). I agree with Salah Ali on this point: my happiness is *my* responsibility, and I don't think there's much that any government can do to further my pursuit of it, other than simply not hindering it with burdensome regulations, taxation, and so forth.

BAD FEELINGS CAN DO GOOD

In February 2008 I appeared on *The O'Reilly Factor* on the Fox News Channel to discuss Americans' views on happiness, and guest host Laura Ingraham posed the question, "Is happiness overrated?"

My answer, then and now: If happiness is defined as the presence of pleasure and positive emotions and absence of pain and negative emotions in the present moment, then yes, it's overrated—but that's not how I define happiness (more on that shortly). Believe it or not, the absence of hardship actually doesn't correlate as much as you might expect with the levels of happiness reported by people from a diverse array of societies and socioeconomic circumstances around the world. And bad feelings aren't all bad.

When I speak to corporate and college-student audiences, I often say, "Most psychologists try to make you feel better and worry less. I may actually make you feel *worse* and worry *more* today, but it's only because I want to help you get better at identifying and avoiding destructive attitudes and behaviors in yourself and others." A little anxiety can help us to think ahead, to plan better for our futures, and to be mindful and careful about how we go through life. And emotions like guilt and shame, often among the first indicators of a need to think more about our actions, can help us recognize when behaviors are destructive— of ourselves and others—and to make course corrections and amends as appropriate.

Yes, anxiety can be overdone and become debilitating, and emotions like guilt and shame can outlast their usefulness and become destructive in and of themselves. But in today's American culture, I believe that we have more people who aren't anxious enough (about truly important things, like the impacts of their choices on their children's and their country's future), and who aren't feeling enough guilt and shame (about genuinely destructive behaviors) than we have people who are harboring excessive amounts of any of the above emotions. (By the way, genuine feelings of guilt at least suggest a certain fundamental goodness within an individual. I've examined plenty of sociopaths, and you never hear them express genuine guilt feelings.)

Even grief, one of life's most painful emotions—as I'm sure Anna Nicole Smith experienced in the aftermath of her son's death—has its place in a full life. Imagine a life in which those with whom you had spent so many good times could simply disappear from your memory without any ill effects. Just imagine how empty a life like that would be. Yes, like shame, guilt, and anxiety, grief can become chronic and prevent us from finding meaning and joy in life as we move forward from a profound loss. (We've all heard bittersweet stories of elderly spouses dying within days of one another.) But in the aftermath of such a loss, grief can help us to know that we've truly loved and been loved in this life.

FINDING YOUR WELTANSCHAUUNG

So if the purpose of our lives is not to be happy, then what is it? Philosophers and theologians throughout human history have pondered this fundamental question—the quest for the meaning of life—and daunting as it may seem, each of us has to answer it before we can truly understand how to pursue, and to actually achieve, happiness in our lives. Now, I'm many things—a psychologist, a lawyer, a TV personality, a world traveler—but I'm not a theologian, so I can't tell you *the* answer; I can just tell you *my* answer. Dictionary.com defines the word *weltanschauung* (pronounced **velt**-ahn-shou-oong) as "a comprehensive conception or image of the universe and of humanity's relation to it." The following is my weltanschauung, and you need to know it early in this book for two important reasons: (1) it's the root of all of my beliefs about the behaviors that we should be practicing, avoiding, encouraging, and discouraging in life; and (2) if you don't share my answer, you'll need to think about your own answer as you read further.

First, I believe that our lives in this world are not just cosmic accidents. I believe that there's a creator (and I derive that belief from secular logic rather than the dictate of any particular faith), that there's a purpose to our lives on this planet, that it's a benevolent purpose, and that there's life after this life (at least potentially, depending perhaps on how we live this life). I cringe, though, whenever I'm involved in media coverage of, for example, a natural disaster story, and the survivors say things on camera like, "I just thank God for sparing our home," as though the creator had chosen which families deserved to have their homes destroyed or spared. I don't believe it works that way, and while I realize that traumatized disaster victims probably don't intend to imply that God doesn't care as much about families whose homes were destroyed, that implication is there. I believe, instead, that many things that understandably seem profound in the context of a human lifespan, like the loss of a home, probably simply aren't as profound in the context of eternity. (For me personally, this concept has been a powerful grief antidote in the aftermath, for example, of my father's passing in 2009. I believe I'll see him again, and though it may take decades in "Earth time," it'll be an instant from now in "eternity time.")

With that as a preamble, here's my answer to the question "What is the *purpose* of our lives?" *To relate to our creator.* I believe that we exist because we have the unique ability not just to amuse or glorify our creator, as beautiful flowers or brilliantly plumed birds might do, but to actually understand and appreciate our creator. How do we do that? I believe we do it in two essential ways: (1) by creating—new people (i.e., becoming parents), new ideas, new images, new sounds, new things—by taking stock of the unique skills, abilities, talents, or gifts inherent in our DNA and developing those as fully as we're able, and in doing so, developing the fullness of our human potential; and (2) by caring—for others, our families, our communities, the needy among us—giving of ourselves to help others to develop the fullness of their potentials. In these ways, we get a glimpse of what it's like to be our creator. We're not forced to make these efforts; if we were, our actions would be meaningless. Instead, we're given the choice, the unique free will, to make them or not, and it's in our choosing that our actions gain meaning. Whether a behavior promotes or hinders these efforts, then, is what distinguishes for me productive from destructive behavior—good from evil—in human relations.

What does this all mean with regard to happiness? It's okay to want to be happy (if you wanted to be sad, I'd be concerned about you), but if we focus on pursuing happiness as the goal of our lives, as an end-state of extrinsic gratification—the presence of pleasure and absence of pain in the here and now—we're less likely to catch and hold onto it. If, instead, we focus on pursuing our life's purpose, on creating and caring, we're actually more likely to catch and hold onto happiness as a byproduct of that pursuit—as profound intrinsic gratification, a deep and lasting sense of meaning. Even if you disagree with me on the metaphysical aspects of why we should create and care in this life, even if you still think we're here *just* "to be happy," there's ample evidence that those who catch and hold onto happiness tend to pursue it as a byproduct of meaning.

From the path to "self-actualization" depicted by noted psychologist Abraham Maslow in 1943; to the path to "ego integrity," depicted by another noted psychologist, Erik Erikson, in 1950; to a rapidly growing body of more recent data compiled by Martin Seligman and other contemporary "positive psychology" researchers, a recurring theme is that we're happiest when we feel we've reached our potential by identifying and using our abilities to contribute something uniquely good to the human condition, when we feel that our lives are meaningful—more than enjoyable, more than comfortable. It turns out that happiness rooted in meaning not only is more lasting, more adversity-resistant—as Seligman describes it, more "authentic"—but it also correlates better with good physical (as well as mental) health than does happiness rooted in pleasure.

So, we need to turn the pursuit of happiness inside out. Many Americans today are pursuing it "outside in." They're looking primarily *outside* of themselves for people and things that supposedly will fill them with happiness when, in fact, they need to be looking primarily inside of themselves for what they have that's uniquely good to put out into the world. In other words, they need to stop *moaning* about the amount of happiness in their lives and start *owning* it!

Yet, instead of creating things and caring *for* others, many Americans who moan about not being happy remain focused on getting things *from* others. . . .

CHAPTER 2

But I Want _____!

All I want is what I have coming to me.

All I want is my fair share.

—Sally Brown,
in *A Charlie Brown Christmas*

ACCESS TO EXCESS

Early on the morning of Black Friday, November 28, 2008, roughly 2,000 shoppers lined up outside of a New York Walmart store, many of them presumably there to buy gifts on sale in celebration of the birth of Jesus Christ, but as I later recounted in a column titled, "You Call This *Christmas* Shopping?" on WorldNetDaily, the behavior that ensued was far from Christ-like. Impatient for the store to open, the crowd eventually forced open its front doors and rushed inside, trampling thirty-four-year-old seasonal employee Jdimytai Damour to death. It wasn't that the first shoppers to enter the store had no choice but to keep moving forward, propelled uncontrollably by the throng of shoppers behind them. Many coldly, callously, literally ran roughshod over Damour and several other people. They even shoved and shouted at Damour's coworkers who attempted to pull him to safety. And as I discussed on national TV that evening, the psychology of herd behavior provided at best a partial explanation. Even if they were caught up in the fervor of an emotionally charged crowd, one might still have expected that shoppers who were shopping with thoughts of Jesus even remotely on their minds would've been jolted out of their herd mentality by a human being dying at their feet, but no. So why not?

In 2011 I appeared on Fox News Channel's daytime program *Happening Now* to discuss Americans' burgeoning appetites—not just for food, but also for material items, often of similarly fleeting value, and for the consumer credit used to obtain such items beyond buyers' means. Host Jon Scott asked me whether I thought there was a connection between Americans' growing waistlines (the Centers for Disease Control now estimate that 35 percent of American adults and 17 percent of American children are obese) and growing credit-card balances (in 2014, American Household Credit Card Debt Statistics put the average American household's outstanding credit card balance at $15,270!). My answer: An unequivocal "yes." In addition to moaning about not having as much happiness as they think they should have, many Americans these days are moaning about not having as many *things* as they think they should have.

In part, this is a byproduct of America's prolonged prosperity, which I dubbed "access to excess." Americans, individually and collectively, have become so accustomed to having not only their needs but also many of their wants fulfilled that they've often conflated the two. Thus, they've come to expect many of their wants to be fulfilled (and all too often, as we saw in the case of their happiness, by others), even as they've behaved less like the previous generations of Americans whose hard work and relative frugality laid the foundations for their prosperity. The results have been destructive in terms of the nation's physical and financial health. And when people want things so badly that they start to objectify their fellow human beings as mere means to material ends, it's perhaps the single most dangerous attitude in the whole of human relations, leading to historical atrocities like slavery, crimes like rape and murder, and disgusting displays of malignant materialism, like the trampling in that New York Walmart back in 2008.

But it's not just that Americans want things—it's that they want things *right now*! In other words, ours hasn't just become a culture that highly prioritizes material gratification; it has become a culture that highly prioritizes *instant* material gratification. In the 1960s and 1970s, Stanford psychologist Walter Mischel conducted a series of experiments involving children's ability (although "ability" isn't really the right word—everyone has the "ability" if it's important enough to them) to delay gratification. The focal point of Mischel's experiments was what has become known as the "marshmallow test," in which kids each were offered a marshmallow to enjoy immediately but were promised a second marshmallow if they refrained from eating the first marshmallow for several minutes.[10] The rewards varied—from marshmallows to other kinds of edible treats—and so did the results. Some kids almost reflexively chose the immediate single reward over the delayed double reward. Others chose to forgo the single reward initially but gave in before the prescribed time passed to receive the double reward. Still others, approximately 30 percent, chose to forgo the single reward and waited as long as it took, generally around fifteen minutes, to successfully claim the double reward.

Percentage of Kids Who "Passed" Mischel's Original "Marshmallow Test"

(Delayed gratification for the full 15 min.)

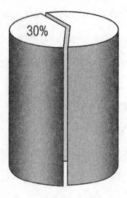

Since then, the results of the marshmallow test have been correlated favorably—by Mischel and his colleagues and others, including some as far away as New Zealand[11]—with various measures of success and health later in life, in areas such as SAT scores, academic achievement, income, attainment of long-term goals, weight control, marital longevity, substance use, and law-abiding tendencies. These correlations persist even across cultures and socioeconomic circumstances.

The Likelihoods of Certain Adolescent and Adult Outcomes as Predicted by Passing the Marshmallow Test

⬆ SAT scores—up

⬆ Academic achievement—up

⬆ Income—up

⬆ Attainment of long-term goals—up

⬇ Weight—down

⬇ Divorce—down

⬇ Substance abuse—down

⬇ Crime—down

YOU OWE ME!

And it's not just that Americans want things, or even that they want things right now. It's that, too often, they feel they're actually owed things! Dictionary.com defines "owe" as "to be under obligation to pay or repay." But if you ask individual Americans what they believe they're "owed" in life, you'll get a wide range of answers. Some will answer that they're owed the freedom to pursue happiness. Others will answer that they're owed basic material "essentials," like food, clothing, and shelter, without which, they'll argue, they can't pursue happiness. Others still will answer that they're owed assistance in their pursuits of happiness, like education, jobs, and health care. Still others, as we saw in Chapter 1, will answer that they're actually owed happiness itself. While all 300 million–plus of us will never agree on what's "essential" in life, nor on what we're "owed," historically speaking, most reasonable Americans have agreed that we're not owed nonessential material things—until recently.

Alarming numbers of Americans seem to be seeing few if any limits to what they're owed. In the first of a two-part series of columns for WorldNetDaily in 2009, I recited a litany of examples: twenty-somethings who took six years (sometimes more) to earn bachelor's degrees, racking up five-figure credit-card debt (not to mention student loans) along the way, then moaning about having to wait to afford luxuries like designer clothes and big-screen televisions that "other people" had (never mind that other people had worked harder, educated themselves better, and saved longer); forty-somethings who were all too eager to take out subprime mortgages and buy homes far beyond their means, then moan about "predatory" lenders when they couldn't make their payments; even sixty-somethings who—despite having been raised by the generation that made some of the greatest sacrifices of any in American history (the WWII or "Greatest" Generation)—were unwilling to sacrifice luxuries for savings during their earning years, voluntarily joined the estimated 14 percent of American adults over sixty-five (36 percent of all American adults over eighteen) who have $0 saved for retirement, and then moan about having to either continue working into their seventies and eighties or to subsist on Social Security payments, with bitter indignation either way.

In that same series of columns, I also recited a litany of ways, other than just financially, in which such Americans' beliefs about what they're "owed" have hurt them: psychologically, professionally, and interpersonally. People who believe they're owed things tend to moan and be jealous and resentful of others who appear to have better possessions, better positions, even "better" people in their lives (the latter reflecting that particularly dangerous *objectification* of human beings that I warned about earlier—more on that coming up), yet neither jealousy nor resentment tends to facilitate the formation of healthy relationships or to improve existing relationships. Successful relationships require mutual sacrifice, yet people who believe they're owed things often expect sacrifice from others without expecting to reciprocate, creating mutual resentment that can damage relationships.

WHAT ABOUT *MY* NEEDS?

To illustrate this point, in the second season of *Fatal Vows*, we did an episode on Sherri and Michael Dally. Michael had showered Sherri with affection and gifts during their courtship but, once married, holding down a job as a night stocker at a grocery store was about the extent of his ambition to support Sherri and the two kids they eventually had. In addition to being lazy, Michael was hypercritical of Sherri, abused substances on a regular basis, and had a wandering eye. For years, Sherri worked tirelessly to provide a second income for the family, keep their home neat and clean, cook Michael's favorite meals, and make herself more physically attractive to him. In short, Sherri was making all of the sacrifices to make the marriage work while Michael was making none.

Eventually, Sherri grew a backbone and became righteously resentful of how Michael had been treating her and their kids. But rather than feeling guilty and changing his ways, Michael equally (though irrationally) became resentful of Sherri's newly asserted expectations that he start behaving like a husband and father. Instead of owning up and manning up, he doubled down on his dereliction of his duties to his family. Given that it was a *Fatal Vows* episode, it's no surprise that their marriage ended in murder (although if you ever get a chance to watch that episode, you may be surprised by who got murdered and who did it!). But as is often the case with our show, the extreme example highlights a far more common problem—in this case, one partner's chronically unreciprocated sacrifice—that portends the death of many relationships, if not the participants themselves.

That same attitude damages professional relationships as well as personal ones. One of my management consulting clients likes to say to recent college graduates, "Ask not what the company can do for you; ask first what you can do for the company!"—an admonition born of his frustration with fresh-out-of-college hires expecting advancement and raises before proving their value to the company. He recently told me about one young employee in particular who had been on the job just three weeks before asking a supervisor when it would be appropriate for them to discuss the employee's first raise. From my client's point of view, a new hire represents an investment of the company's money and training in someone who's likely to take up to a year to learn the job, learn how the company works, and then—hopefully—start generating a return on that investment. To my client, this particular young man was frustratingly representative of those young Americans I discussed in Chapter 1—the ones who've esteemed themselves such that they've moaned about their work not being valued highly enough and rewarded progressively enough despite its quality—neither appropriately self-critical nor appreciative of others' constructive criticism. And when one fails to identify one's weaknesses, improvement, and therefore advancement, are difficult.

In the summer of 2015, Lee Siegel wrote a column in the *New York Times* entitled "Why I Defaulted on My Student Loans."[12] Siegel wrote about how financially strapped his parents had been and about how he had taken out his first student loan at age seventeen to attend "a small private liberal arts college"—which apparently was the prestigious and expensive Columbia University.[13] After taking out another loan and finishing a second year there, he transferred to a less expensive state school but then dropped out and worked briefly in retail before returning, apparently to Columbia, and borrowing more money, apparently a lot more money, because this time, he stayed long enough to finish not only a bachelor's degree but also two master's degrees. Siegel acknowledged that he could've stayed at the less expensive school but wrote that he "deserved better." He also acknowledged that he could've gotten a job thereafter that would've enabled him to make his student loan payments but wrote that he shouldn't have had to spend his "precious young life" doing a job that didn't recognize or reward his "particular usefulness to society," which—at least *he* thinks—is writing.

Siegel blamed everyone from financial entities (for having the audacity to try to actually collect the money he owed) to the wealthy, to the government, to society at large for his decision to simply stop making the payments, and for that decision, he was unapologetic. In fact, he encouraged young borrowers to consider following his example and even offered them tips on how they might avoid some of the ensuing financial fallout—tips such as, "Get as many credit cards as you can before your credit is ruined," and, "Live with or marry someone with good credit." (Here's a tip from me: You *never* want to be married to anyone who's such a user—such a *loser*—that their motivation to be with you has anything to do with your good credit!)

The attitude that one is owed things implies that there must be another person—or group, institution, community, or nation— who owes one those things, and that attitude can be used to rationalize all kinds of taking behaviors. Along with a tendency to delay gratification or not, most of the major ground rules for healthy human relations ("Don't hit someone who isn't hitting you," "Be honest," "Pick up after yourself," and "You can't just take whatever you want from whomever you want whenever you want it") tend to be internalized, or not, early in life. Their internalization, or not, also tends to be fairly well correlated. In other words, when people fail to internalize a tendency to delay gratification, they often also fail to internalize a number of those other lessons. A shoplifter, for example, is someone who clearly hasn't internalized a tendency to delay gratification. They don't want to wait until they can afford what they want; they want it *now*. But they also clearly haven't internalized a value of others' property rights, and if you asked them where they got whatever it is that they've shoplifted, you'll probably find that they haven't internalized a value of honesty either.

A person who makes it even to late adolescence, and certainly to adulthood, without having internalized such values is a person who's unlikely to consider the long-term impacts of their actions in general and particularly the long- and short-term impacts of their actions upon others. Psychologists call such individuals *antisocial*, which has nothing to do with disinterest in socializing (that's *avoidant*) and everything to do with a lack of empathy, and it's virtually always traceable back to one's childhood. Sometimes that childhood is shown to have been overindulgent. Other times, it turns out to have been the opposite: profoundly neglectful. Interestingly, both of those paths can lead to the same place in life. Self-aggrandizement and self-pity both can produce an excessive focus on one's own needs and wants, which is often accompanied by a sense of being *owed* those needs and wants.

CALIBRATING THE MORAL COMPASS

Individuals who feel that they're owed things in life tend to become net "takers" (as opposed to net "givers" or even "reciprocators"), and as that tendency approaches its extreme, it may be limited only by what they think they can get away with. In such extreme cases, it's as if the individuals became fixated in the preconventional stage of moral development, as described by developmental psychologist Lawrence Kohlberg in the 1950s and '60s. In that stage, which is supposed to span just the first couple of years of one's life, children's motivation to regulate their behavior is almost exclusively extrinsic. That is, whether they engage in a behavior is determined simply by what they expect to gain versus what they expect to lose as a result. In a healthy developmental process, though, the individual passes on to a *conventional* stage, in which they internalize a respect for rules and a tendency toward conformity. Then they ultimately progress to a *postconventional* level, in which they internalize a reasoned set of intrinsic values (e.g., respect for others as well as for themselves) that largely govern their behavior thereafter. A person who remains primarily extrinsically motivated into adulthood is one whose concepts of right and wrong are rooted primarily in the consequences that they'll likely experience if they engage in or avoid certain behaviors. In other words, life's all about them. The only way to get them to do the objectively right thing is to make it in their own selfish best interests to do so, which, in practice, requires omnipresent observation by an authority equipped to administer sufficiently motivating rewards or punishments in real time. If you get a chance to ask such people, they'll even tell you as much.

A few years ago I was asked to be an examining expert on behalf of a medical licensing board that was investigating a surgeon who had received a second citation for driving under the influence of alcohol (DUI). The board wanted to know whether this doctor had an alcohol problem and whether I thought it might be spilling over into his professional practice. When I met with the doctor, he was arrogant, flippant, and clearly irritated about having to come to my office. He assured me that he wasn't an alcoholic and minimized his two DUIs as the results of overzealous policing by officers who had nothing better to do than to pull him over for slightly exceeding the speed limit on his way home from having a few drinks with friends, even though he said he was fine to drive. He even speculated that the police had profiled him because he drove a fancy sports car. Then he assured me that he'd learned his lesson about drinking and driving, that he'd never get another DUI, and that the medical board would never again have cause for concern about his drinking.

I asked him how he could be so sure, and as he rattled off reasons for his certainty, I wrote them down on a chalkboard in my office. Here was his list:

- "My name's already been in the newspaper for this once— if it happens again, I'll lose patients."
- "I'll lose my license to drive for a year, even to and from work."

- "The board will suspend my medical license and make me pay for rehab whether I'm really an alcoholic or not."
- "My partners might kick me out of our practice."
- "I won't be able to afford my car and house payments."
- "My wife says if I get another DUI, she'll divorce me."

Notice what I noticed? It was all about *him*. I asked him—twice—whether he could think of anything to add to his list, and he couldn't. Only then did I point out to him—as I explained my rationale for recommending the suspension of his license to practice medicine—that nowhere on his list was there any reference to the possibility that he could've hurt someone or orphaned his kids and widowed his wife. His lack of empathy would've been appalling coming from anyone, but especially from a surgeon, whose job is to repair bodies on surgical tables, not put them there!

Even when they appear to be successful in the short term, as that doctor did, such individuals typically don't do very well in the long term, leaving behind a trail of hurt people from whom they've taken and taken and taken. *You* can take *this* from me, though: just as you don't ever want to be married to a person like that, you don't ever want to be in business with a person like that. Their belief that they're owed things makes it easier for them to rationalize and justify satisfying their professional as well as personal wants in dishonest and destructive ways. It's as if their moral compass becomes like Captain Jack Sparrow's compass in *Pirates of the Caribbean*, pointing not necessarily to what's right but simply to whatever its bearer most wants.

People who believe they're owed rewards before establishing commensurate track records of excellence in their job performance are more likely to employ unethical or even illegal tactics to acquire those rewards—particularly when they're in competition with peers who excel through superior ability or work ethic—thus jeopardizing their jobs, their reputations, and even their freedom. Just weeks before this book went to press, a New York book-keeper was arrested for allegedly stealing a seven-figure sum of money from his comatose employer and, when caught, claiming he was *owed* the money because he hadn't been given salary raises that he thought he deserved![14] The fact is, cases ranging from outright theft to identity theft to the complex embezzlement and fraud schemes that have led to numerous financially devastat-ing corporate scandals in recent years all reflect the perpetrators' beliefs that they're owed things—beliefs that, as we've seen, tend to take root early in life.

In late 1998 Ajay Mathew Thomas appeared to be on his way to a successful life, honing formidable information technology (IT) skills while earning Bs at one of the most rigorous univer-sities in the world, Harvard. But Bs weren't good enough for Thomas, who wanted a job as a clerk for a federal judge. So what did he do? Study more? No, when it came time to apply for jobs, Thomas used his IT skills to change several of the Bs on his Har-vard transcript to As. In early 1999, someone from the university detected the tampering and questioned Thomas about it, where-upon Thomas assured the employee that "it was all a joke" and that he would use his real transcript when applying for jobs. The very next day, Thomas applied for clerkships with twenty-three federal judges—using the falsified transcript. But the university was onto him, and disciplinary proceedings were convened. What did Thomas do then? Come clean and beg for a second chance?

No, he lied again. Thomas told university officials that he had falsified his transcript solely to impress his parents and that the forgery had been included with his job applications by mistake. They didn't buy it. Thomas was expelled.

What was his next move? Did he apply to other schools and try to complete his education honestly? No, he used his IT skills to create a dummy company called Computer Data Forensics that then supposedly "recovered" electronic evidence corroborating his failed defense, which he then used to appeal his expulsion. It almost worked. In light of the new "evidence," Harvard reconsidered Thomas's expulsion but ultimately upheld it.

What then? Did Thomas finally learn his lesson and try to piece his shattered future back together as best he could? No, he changed his name to Mathew Martoma and got a high-paying job—using what credentials we may never know—at a hedge fund called SAC Capital. But that still wasn't enough for him. He obtained inside information from a physician about the development of a drug to treat Alzheimer's disease and illegally used that information to make investments that generated over $200 million for SAC Capital and over $9 million for himself. Once again, he got caught.

So did he come clean this time and try to set things right? (Surely you don't expect that by now!) No, he refused to admit wrongdoing and fought the Securities and Exchange Commission and federal prosecutors tooth and nail. Partly because of his utter lack of remorse, in late 2014, then age forty and married with three children, he received one of the toughest sentences ever handed down for an insider trading conviction, a fine of over $9 million and a nine-year prison term. Yet when asked about the

transcript forgery at Harvard back when he was Ajay Mathew
Thomas, a spokesperson for Mathew Martoma said, "This event
of fifteen years ago is entirely unrelated to—and has no bearing
on—this case."

While you never want to be married to or in business with
someone like that, even more importantly, you never want to raise
someone like that. I worry, though, that American parents are
raising more Mathew Martomas today than ever before. In an
anonymous survey of thousands of American teenagers in 2008,[15]
over 30 percent admitted to having stolen something from a store
in the prior year, yet over 90 percent expressed satisfaction with
themselves in terms of ethics and character. It's frightening to
realize that those 30 percent, especially if they're representative of
their generation, are now out there somewhere in our workforce,
perhaps even in your workplace. More frightening is the reality
that small-time takers tend to grow into big-time takers, like Martoma did. Even more frightening is the prospect of a company
with a significant percentage of aspiring Mathew Martomas in
its ranks. And even still *more* frightening is a stock market with a
significant percentage of such companies factoring into its value!

Beliefs that people are owed things wreak havoc not just on
marriages and careers but on families and children, too. Husbands and wives who believe that their spouses and families owe
them happiness (which, by the way, is almost always evident during courtship, if one's eyes are open) aren't just more likely to
cheat, as we saw in the *Fatal Vows* case of Michael Dally; they're
also more likely to shirk their responsibilities to support their
dependents, as we saw in the cases of Dally and Martoma, both
of whom went off to prison.

In addition, parents who believe that their children owe them affection tend to treat those children like pets, thinking more about what they (the parents) want *from* the children rather than what they owe *to* the children. One of the characters who has appeared again and again in the news stories I've covered over the years has been Nadya Suleman, better known as "Octomom." She used in vitro fertilization to have a total of fourteen children (eight in a single pregnancy, hence her moniker), and when she couldn't support them consistently, she (allegedly) resorted to welfare fraud. I've found Octomom so appallingly representative of everything that's gone wrong with American parenting that while her octuplets were still infants, I once proposed, on national television, actually going ahead and giving her what she seemed to have wanted all along—a reality TV show—but calling it *Adoption Idol* and letting decent, self-sacrificing, stable, married couples compete for the opportunity to adopt her kids. One of the hardest things for me to witness as a psychologist has been parents repeatedly putting what *they* want—material wealth, drugs and alcohol, sex, and so on—ahead of what their children *need*. The damage that I've seen done to the children has been immeasurable, and given the poor parental models that those children have had, the damage is often cyclical, although it doesn't have to be.

GENERATION TAKE?

In some ways I worry that we're becoming a *nation* of takers. While the story of Robin Hood has been celebrated in our American culture and parents have read the story to children for generations, the story makes me cringe because, at its core, it's essentially an ends-justify-the-means tale that I think blurs an important distinction between envy and jealousy and contributes more to people's moral confusion than to healthy moral development.

Envy is the desire to also have what someone else has, and envy can be a perfectly healthy emotion if it prompts one to make oneself more productive in order to replicate someone else's good fortune. *Jealousy*, however, is the desire to exclusively have what someone else has—that is, to take for oneself what belongs to someone else. Jealousy is almost always an unhealthy emotion.

The shoplifters I discussed earlier in this chapter, for example, generally didn't want to go to the trouble to work hard and be able to also have something that belonged to someone else; no, they wanted to just take it so that it belonged to them instead of to someone else. At the extreme, we've seen time and time again on *Fatal Vows* people going so far as to commit murder in an effort to clear a path to someone else's spouse!

It's also troubling to see politicians essentially validating jealousy via campaign rhetoric and then reinforcing jealousy via public policy. We've been hearing a lot from American politicians in recent years about the need to address "income inequality," language that falsely implies that something is inherently wrong with some people having more, even far more, than others, and that many Americans aren't getting as much as they deserve.

My favorite TV Christmas special of all time is *A Charlie Brown Christmas*. In that classic cartoon, Charlie's sister, Sally, epitomizes the reason for his despair about the overcommercialization of Christmas when she moans, in defense of her lengthy list of desired gifts, "All I want is what's coming to me. All I want is my fair share." Those last two little words of Sally's—"fair" and "share"—have become big buzzwords of American political rhetoric in recent years. One of the most frequent uses of "fair share" involves accusing higher-earning Americans of not bearing their fair share of the nation's tax burden, when, according to the Internal Revenue Service, the top 10 percent of earners actually bear over two-thirds of that burden (with the bottom 50 percent of earners assuming just 3 percent of it). In fact, if we really wanted to parse Americans' "fair shares" of the tax burden, my fellow pundit Adam Corolla walked us through those calculations on a 2012 episode of *The O'Reilly Factor*: $3.8 trillion (the federal budget at the time) divided by the population (about 318 million at the time) worked out to just over $12,000 per person.

So, if we actually charged each American the same annual fee for the privilege of membership in our great nation, then those paying less than $12,000 per year in federal taxes (which includes everyone in that bottom 50 percent of earners) would actually be the ones paying less than their fair shares. Now, as a practical matter, we couldn't come close to getting $12,000 per year from most Americans, nor could we come close to running our society (at least not in the way that we've been running it for generations) if we really charged each American an annual fee that they *could* all afford to pay, but we never seem to hear anything about the fair share of the nearly *half* of all American adults who pay no federal income tax whatsoever yet still receive all of the benefits of American citizenship. Similarly, we hear a lot of moaning about how "greedy" it is for higher earners to oppose having more of their incomes redistributed to lower earners via various tax-supported public assistance programs, but we never hear any moaning about how greedy it is to take assistance from those programs if a person is mentally and physically capable of meeting his or her own needs in life (which the vast majority of adults actually are—more in Chapter 6).

According to data released by the U.S. Census Bureau, in 2012 over one-third of Americans, approximately 110 million, were receiving some form of means-tested government benefits (i.e., not including elderly recipients of Social Security and Medicare benefits). At that time, over 51 million Americans were receiving food stamps; approximately 83 million were receiving healthcare benefits through Medicaid; 22.5 million were receiving benefits from the Women, Infants, and Children (WIC) program; 20.4 million were receiving Supplemental Security Income (SSI); 13.3 million were receiving public housing or housing subsidies; and 5.4 million were receiving Temporary Assistance to Needy Families (TANF). These figures don't include the estimated 6 to 7 million Americans who have since begun to receive health insurance subsidies under the Affordable Care Act, and millions of Americans are recipients of benefits from two or more of the foregoing programs simultaneously. There's simply no way, in my estimation, that one-third of Americans are mentally or physically incapable of being productive enough to fulfill their own basic needs or the basic needs of their offspring, which means there are an awful lot of Americans moaning for assistance they'd do without if they had to. If you add in elderly Americans receiving Social Security retirement income and healthcare benefits through the Medicare program, plus veterans receiving veterans' benefits, by 2014, over half of Americans were receiving some form of government benefits. For the first time in our nation's history, more people were receiving benefits than were funding those benefits. The elderly and the veterans are not takers; they paid into those programs— senior citizens with earnings over the course of their working lives and veterans with their service to the nation—but funding the benefits legitimately owed to them while also funding benefits to another third of the population simply isn't sustainable.

When people aren't moaning about what their fellow Americans owe them, they're often moaning about what their employers owe them. Even though, for example, most employees would be righteously indignant if they put in a day's work for no pay, many nevertheless moan for the government to force their employers to pay them a day's wages for no work if they get sick and miss a day, *and* to pay for their health insurance so they don't have to spend any of the missed day's wages on a doctor visit. And during the 2012 presidential campaign, Sandra Fluke, a law student at the time, got famous by moaning for the government to force employers to pay not just for prescription medications, chemicals to promote healthy physiological functioning, but even for contraceptives, chemicals to prevent healthy physiological functioning. (How a soon-to-be-lawyer reasoned that employers should be forced to facilitate their employees' recreational sex was, and still is, beyond me. If one's not mature enough to secure one's own contraception and to fulfill eighteen years' worth of an unplanned child's needs, then one's not mature enough for sex. Yet she succeeded, so I guess if I were smart, I'd just be glad to know that we men must now similarly be owed employer-paid condoms!) Is it any wonder why many American job creators have chosen in recent years to earn and keep their money outside of the United States?

IT TAKES A THIEF

Americans' sense of what they're owed has seemingly spiraled out of control. There's a line in the 2008 movie *Iron Man* in which the villain moans to the hero, "You really think that because you have an idea, it belongs to you?" Sounds pretty villainous, right? Right, yet millions of Americans don't seem to see themselves as villainous when they confiscate other people's intangible property by, for example, illegally downloading songs, games, and pirated copies of movies like *Iron Man*. And as an attorney, I am particularly troubled to see even those whose jobs ostensibly require judicious balancing of rights—like judges and public officials—increasingly accepting arguments that Americans are owed things that they're really not owed at all.

For example, in 2015 the U.S. Army decided that it was cruel and unusual punishment not to fund sex-change procedures for a convicted leaker of national security secrets who moaned that he'd rather serve the remainder of his thirty-five-year sentence in the women's disciplinary barracks at Fort Leavenworth instead of in the men's. Now, the reason he was in jail for leaking data was, according to him, that he had to hide his identity because of the military's "Don't ask, don't tell" policy in effect at that time. He claimed the depression and stress caused him to steal and leak the data. The inmate then took it a step further and claimed that the sex reassignment procedures were necessary treatment for gender dysphoria, but they're not. Nobody *needs* sex-change procedures because they feel "dysphoria"—that is, unhappiness—about their genders. It's nice that the army doesn't want to inflict cruel and unusual punishment on a prisoner. I just wish it were equally loath to inflict cruel and unusual punishment on us taxpayers!

Meanwhile, as multiple states are taking steps to decriminalize marijuana use, the city of Berkeley, California, has taken that idea a step further and is making medicinal marijuana available *free* to low-income "patients" who moan that it's too expensive. And by the way, nobody needs to smoke "medicinal" marijuana; the pain-relieving compound in marijuana can be administered in a prescription drug that actually delivers a *therapeutic* dose of that pain reliever, which is extremely difficult to measure in smoke form, *without* getting one high. Life really does appear to be imitating art as alarming numbers of Americans seem to be falling through Lewis Carroll's looking glass (the portal through which Alice traveled to Wonderland in 1865) and making the 2006 movie *Idiocracy*—about a futuristic America in which the inmates run not just the asylum but everything else, too—seem frighteningly plausible.

GIVE OR TAKE A TRILLION

As Americans' sense of what they're owed has spiraled out of control, so has our federal budget. As of 2015 the United States' national debt had topped $18 trillion and was growing at the rate of around $1 trillion annually (due to interest on existing debt plus new borrowing; for example, in 2016 we're projected to collect around $3.5 trillion in taxes and spend around $4 trillion). To bring those figures down to Earth, imagine an individual American who'll earn $35,000 this year yet spend $40,000, adding $5,000 to his existing debt of $180,000, on which interest is constantly compounding. By the end of the year, he'll be in debt to the tune of about $190,000, yet he plans to repeat this pattern again, year after year, indefinitely into the future. The problem is it's simply unsustainable. In fact, if we were talking about an individual American earning $35,000 per year and owing $180,000, even with overly loose credit and rampant abuses thereof, he'd likely have had a hard time finding lenders willing to lend him more money, certainly on any realistically acceptable terms, well before now.

The difference in the nation's case is that it can print its own money, so in theory, as long as its debt is owed in its own currency, the country will always be able to pay the debt back. But it's not that simple. We know from economics and history that when a nation tries to solve its debt problem simply by printing money, the value of that money drops, often precipitously, causing hyperinflation problems that have ultimately collapsed such nations' economies. So, while our collective pattern of indulging on borrowed money may be more sustainable than similar patterns among individual Americans, it's still ultimately unsustainable. Practically speaking, just as individual Americans have to do, we're ultimately going to have to tighten our collective belt and live more within our national means. Our only practical choice, then, is whether we want to start cutting back sooner, while we still can do it gradually and avoid causing acute suffering, particularly among our more vulnerable citizens, or whether we want to wait until we simply can't borrow any more, at which point we'll have to do it rapidly, less discriminately, and more painfully. The preferable option is obvious to me, but given how we seem to have ceded both our culture and our country to short-term gratification seekers, it's tough to be optimistic that we're going to change our fiscal course until we're forced to do so.

YOU BELONG TO ME

At their most extreme, people's beliefs that they're owed things can be dangerous. Depending on the depth of one's belief that one's wants are deserved, challenging that belief can elicit the kind of anger that leads to abusive, violent, even deadly behavior of the type that we spotlight on *Fatal Vows*. In 2014 the FBI arrested an Indiana man for threatening to kill Speaker of the House John Boehner because Boehner didn't support extending unemployment benefits beyond two years (more on that in Chapter 5). Similarly, though lethally this time, in 2012, as law enforcement officers went to the door of a Texas residence to deliver an eviction notice, the deadbeat tenant opened fire on the officers, killing an officer and a bystander and wounding several others before officers shot him dead. The murderer's mother later told the media that her son's "illness" had caused the tragedy, but I didn't buy it. I'm sure her son wasn't the mentally healthiest guy in town, but it looked (and still looks) to me like he essentially felt like he was owed a house, rent or no rent, for as long as he wanted—so much so that he felt justified in killing anyone who tried to dislodge him. Then in 2015, the adult son of a wealthy New York hedge fund manager was arrested and charged with murdering his father because he apparently threatened to reduce the son's allowance. Now, no one's to blame for the father's murder but the murderer. However, if the father was still giving his adult son an allowance, I can see how he may inadvertently have also raised a son who felt so narcissistic, so sociopathic, so profoundly owed as to become violent when his presumed fair share of the father's earnings was reduced.

People's beliefs that they're owed things don't necessarily stop at inanimate things—objects, like money and houses—either. In fact, such beliefs become most dangerous when they extend to the objectification of human beings. On *Fatal Vows* we've featured sad case after sad case in which people have felt that they were owed the continued possession of ex-spouses, using "If-I-can't-have-her/him-nobody-can!" as a rationale for murder. And every time I think I've heard the worst behavior that people can exhibit, something else comes along to raise the bar of disgust and disbelief. Back in 2013, a Pennsylvania couple used an Internet sex-for-hire ad to lure an unsuspecting young man into their car, where they then strangled and stabbed him to death, simply—based on the husband's statements to police—because they were owed a chance to experience what it felt like to kill someone. That's psychopathy, and the human mind doesn't get any more dangerous.

LIVING IN A MATERIAL WORLD

The truth is, we're *not* owed much, if anything, beyond the basics—life, liberty, and the pursuit of happiness. Yet, the perception and assertion that we're owed access to excess is fueling dysfunction, distress, and downright destruction at all levels of American society. Expanding waistlines and expanding credit-card balances are damaging people's physical and financial health, as evidenced by the fact that people are heading to furniture stores in droves to buy something called a "chair-and-a-half"—on credit!

Dishonest behaviors such as infidelity and fraud are damaging people's relationships and careers. Taken to the extreme, a sense of being owed essentially forms the core of every sociopathic and psychopathic personality I've ever assessed. (Sociopaths are those who've hurt innocent people in the pursuit of other objectives, like robbery, and psychopaths are those for whom hurting innocent people *was* the objective, as in the case of the Pennsylvania couple above who committed murder just for the "fun" of it.) What's worse is that we seem to be socializing kids to believe that they're owed more and more, as evidenced by spoiled brats making national headlines in 2014 suing their parents for everything from a car to college tuition to the startup capital for a pizza franchise.

In 2013 I again appeared on Fox News Channel's *Happening Now* to discuss research on "retail therapy." This is the practice of people—mostly young people—going shopping and buying things in an effort to make themselves feel better. In many cases, they can't really afford these things outright and pay for these wants with credit cards. Then they post happy pictures of themselves on social media, enjoying their trappings of supposed upward mobility, and avoiding the dreaded "downward social comparison" from their social media friends. Of course, this happiness is built on a house of cards—credit cards—and the study found that creating such façades of affluence might mimic happiness, but only briefly. What typically followed were "narcissistic collapses," when those façades crumbled under the pressure of unpaid bills and the inability to keep up with others' (probably similarly exaggerated) exhibitions of "affluence." Focusing on things in those ways ultimately left those young people feeling more disconnected from others and worse about themselves than ever.

There's nothing wrong with wanting material prosperity. It provides security and the opportunity to enjoy an elevated quality of life as well as to help others. When people spend more, it helps fuel the economy, and when people have more disposable income, they have the ability to give more to charity than if they were cash strapped and needed to use their earnings solely to pay for necessities. However, material prosperity, in and of itself, doesn't equal happiness, as those suicidal celebrities from Chapter 1 remind us. There generally also needs to be a consciousness that one is creating things of value to others. Human beings tend to be most prosperous and happiest when they make as much of themselves and earn as much of what they need and want for themselves as possible. So, if we want to maximize the chances for individuals, families, organizations, communities, and the nation to reach the fullness of their potentials both to prosper and to be happy, we each have to get back to expecting less from others and more from ourselves. In other words, we need to stop moaning about what we lack and start owning it!

Yet while many Americans continue to moan about what they *do* want, many also moan about something they *don't* want: accountability for their behavior.

CHAPTER 3

But It's Not My Fault!

> You're like the thief who isn't the least bit sorry he stole,
> but is terribly, terribly sorry he's going to jail.
>
> —Rhett Butler, in *Gone with the Wind*

THE SOCIOPATH'S TOOLBOX

I've been in my share of brawls on talk shows over the years (all verbal—I've never had a fist or a chair thrown at me, as have my colleagues Geraldo Rivera and Jerry Springer, at least not yet!), and my favorite one ever was with celebrity attorney Gloria Allred when she was representing a former mistress of pro golfer Tiger Woods. In what to me was a breathtaking display of how far our culture had sunk, Gloria's argument was that Woods had wronged her client because he had led the young woman to believe that she was his *only* mistress. The client knew that Woods was married, of course, so she knew that he was cheating on his wife; she was just mad because she purportedly thought that she had been the only woman with whom he was cheating. As it turned out, not only had Woods been cheating on his wife; he had also been "cheating" (although I don't think that's technically possible) on the mistress, with multiple other women, over quite some time.

Gloria knows how to brawl, but thanks to the opportunities that I had early in my career (for which I'm always grateful) to study under media masters Nancy Grace and Bill O'Reilly, by this time I could brawl with the best of 'em! Gloria had just finished demanding that Woods apologize to her client (i.e., admit wrongdoing so that she could then demand cash from him) when I broke in and asked, "Has your client apologized to Tiger's wife and kids?" Gloria acted like she suddenly had a bad earpiece and couldn't hear me—and who knows, it was live TV, maybe that's really what happened—which only made me repeat my question, louder this time. Finally Gloria responded, saying that if Woods' then-wife wanted to hear from her client, she [Gloria] would make it happen. And that was the last we heard—the last *I* heard, at least—of the great mistress-scorned case.

But it wasn't the last we heard of Woods's philandering. No, faced with the loss of his marriage, the loss of full-time access to his children, the loss of some high-dollar sponsorships, and the loss of some disgusted fans, he staged a teary-eyed (but utterly disingenuous, it seemed to me) public apology and did what many embattled celebrities do these days to get the heat of the media's spotlights off of themselves for a while: he checked in to rehab.

For what affliction? Addiction. To what? Alcohol? No. Drugs? No. Sex. That's right, he hadn't cheated because he was a famous, materially rich, morally bankrupt pro athlete who had seized opportunities as fast as star-struck and/or gold-digging young women could throw themselves at him. No, he was a victim, a sufferer of a disease that had compelled him to have sex with those women, against his will, and for which he had finally found the courage to seek treatment. How brave of him, right? Wrong.

But these days, a lot of Americans whose names you've never heard are behaving sadly similarly. While they're moaning about not having enough happiness and moaning about not having enough things, you'll never hear them moaning about a lack of accountability for their behavior when the results aren't good. And to avoid that accountability, more and more everyday Americans (and their kids) seem to be using, with varying degrees of skill, what I've found to be the classic blame-evasion tools of sociopaths, which are in the following chart:

Accountability-Avoidance Tools from the Sociopath's Toolbox

TOOL	EXAMPLE
Externalization	"It wasn't me!" "I couldn't control myself!"
Deflection	"Others have done worse!" "If you hadn't done what you did, I wouldn't have done what I did!"
Minimization	"I made a mistake." "I'm only human."

EXTERNALIZATION VIA ADDICTION

A longtime favorite externalization of celebrities and nonce-lebrities alike is addiction, and that term isn't just for substance abuse anymore. As Tiger Woods famously exemplified, we're throwing the word *addiction* around so loosely these days that it can apply to just about anything anyone likes doing enough that they'll continue doing it despite destructive consequences: having sex, gaming (casino or video), eating. . . . Believe it or not, as of 2014, even *sunbathing* supposedly can become an addiction. Harvard researchers found that exposure to ultraviolet light raised endorphins in mice and hypothesized that the same reaction accounts for why so many human beings enjoy sunbathing.[16] But to jump from, "Sunbathing causes a pleasurable chemical reaction in people" to "People are compelled to sunbathe" is a leap too far. Can you imagine having an employee miss work and say, "Sorry, boss, I couldn't help it. My sunbathing addiction forced me to go to the swimming pool instead of working today"?

The truth is we all have things we'd prefer to be doing when instead we need to be working or spending time with our loved ones; we all have things we'd enjoy doing today but that would be harmful to us or our loved ones in the long run. And most of us understand—though understanding it may be easier than practicing it—that we need to regulate and moderate our behavior so as not to indulge in such things, at least not to unhealthy degrees. But here again, some of my colleagues in the healthcare professions have done more harm than good lately, handing Americans a powerful excuse not to self-regulate and instead to overindulge in just about anything. By labeling addictions of various types "diseases," they've semantically transformed character problems into clinical problems, violators (e.g., of marriage vows) into victims, and perpetrators (e.g., of drug crimes) into patients. Tiger Woods has never been teed up more perfectly!

In 2010 the cartoon series *South Park* aired an episode about sex addiction in which various celebrities used that excuse to absolve themselves of accountability for various horrendous sexual behaviors. The "addicts" immediately labeled anyone who questioned the validity of that excuse a "turd in the punch bowl." In that sense, then, I may be the original "turd in the punch bowl" because I've been saying that sex addiction was bogus since the very first time I ever heard those two words uttered sequentially. And in the past couple of years, at least some of my colleagues have caught up with me. A groundbreaking (or, more accurately, myth-busting) study conducted at UCLA in 2013 literally looked into the brains of supposed sex addicts while they viewed erotic images, and guess what? Their brain activity showed *no irregularities*. I'm always happy when colleagues in psychology and the media finally arrive at conclusions that logic dictated (and that I stated) well before—better late than never. Sex addiction is just a lame excuse for narcissists to indulge themselves at others' expense, but even if it were real, it wouldn't excuse anything. Wanting to do something so badly that one is willing to hurt one's family to do it may mean that one has problems psychologically, but it still doesn't mean one can't resist doing the behavior. It just means that one is selfish enough to put one's wants above one's family's needs.

And despite the fact that the American Medical Association chose (against the recommendation of its own study group) in

2013 to label obesity a "disease," overindulgence in food is no more a disease than overindulgence in sex—although both may *result* in diseases. (The AMA's decision may have something to do with the roughly $150 billion charged annually in the United States for healthcare services related to obesity, which will likely balloon thanks to this disease designation, as more insurance plans reimburse more services for more patients.) Simply put, nobody is forced to be overweight. It's an immutable law of physics (the law of "conservation of matter") that mass cannot end up as part of one's body without first entering that body in some other form—that is, food. Yes, there are diseases, like certain thyroid conditions, as well as certain medications that make it harder for some people to regulate their weight than others, because those conditions and medications cause people's bodies to store excess fat, to retain excess water, to feel hungry when they shouldn't, or to be less physically active. But just because something's harder for some people than others, regardless of the reason, doesn't mean it's impossible (more on this in Chapter 6).

I've been to plenty of impoverished areas of the world in which subsets of their populations are affected by the same thyroid conditions to which some Americans attribute their extra weight, and yet the affected individuals in those impoverished areas still aren't overweight. Thus, regulating food intake relative to physical activity, whether involuntary (i.e., due to the constraints of one's circumstances) or voluntary, can, in virtually all cases, keep a person from being obese. Despite genetics, diseases, medications, a concentration of fast-food restaurants (as opposed to healthier eateries) near one's home, or whatever excuses anybody wants to make, it's physically impossible for a human body to grow without consuming more calories than it burns.

Moreover, studies have shown that weight-loss programs (like smoking cessation programs) are more effective when participants are given financial incentives to change their behavior. For example, in 2013, doctors at the Mayo Clinic completed a one-year randomized, controlled clinical trial of financial incentives for weight loss and found that participants who received financial incentives were more than twice as likely to complete their weight-loss programs and lost, on average, more than three times as much weight as participants who didn't receive financial incentives.[17] That really says it all—if one can change for money, then one can change, so the problem's primarily motivational, not medical.

That doesn't mean obese people are bad people, of course. It just means that every adult (I'll address kids shortly) can and must decide what they're willing to give up for what they want. Some are over their ideal weights but still in a healthy weight range, and because of circumstances like systemic or arthritic disease, the time, energy, money, and so on, they'd have to spend in order to attain their ideal weights is time, energy, money, and so on, that they'd prefer to spend with or on their families. If the primary impetus to spend these resources on weight loss would be vanity rather than any significant increase in health or longevity, and they conclude that the required sacrifices aren't worth the potential benefits, you won't hear me criticizing their choices. The only time you'll hear me take issue with them is if they say there's *no* choice involved—that is, they're forced to be overweight. I simply don't believe that, although I have enough empathy to understand how it could be comforting to some people to believe it, which is why you'll hear me directing most of my comments about obesity toward (1) parents who allow their children to become obese, (2) obese adults who expect their fellow Americans to bear health-care costs resulting from their poor dietary choices, and (3) politicians who seek to restrict *everyone's* dietary choices based upon the false premise that we *must* bear such costs collectively.

According to a recent article about supposed addiction to video games, a key symptom is that the "addicted" individual "experiences relapse"—that is, tries unsuccessfully to quit, as if whether to play a video game or not, no matter how badly they may want to play it, isn't 100 percent their choice (or, if we're talking about a minor, their parents' choice).[18] In the context of addictive behavior, I think it's misleading to say that anyone truly "experiences relapse." What they do is quit for a while and then choose (or, if we're talking about a minor, are allowed) to start up again. Addicts of all types tend to like to use the clinical term "relapse," but in my office, it doesn't fly. The dialogue usually goes something like this:

> **Addict:** "I was doing really great with my recovery until I relapsed."
>
> **Me:** "You mean, until you chose to do it again?"
>
> **Addict:** "What do you mean?"
>
> **Me:** "Well, did you know what you were doing?"
>
> **Addict:** "Yeah."
>
> **Me:** "And did anyone force you to do it?"
>
> **Addict:** "No."
>
> **Me:** "So you chose to do it again, did you not?"
>
> **Addict:** "I guess."
>
> **Me:** "See, a woman who had breast cancer in the past and developed a new tumor in her breast relapsed. She didn't choose to start having cancer again. So please, let's not insult her by acting like your situation and hers are similar."

It's easy to see why addicts embrace clinical words like "disease" and "relapse," but in my professional opinion, using such terminology in the context of addiction does a disservice to all concerned. In addition to insulting those suffering from diseases like breast cancer, calling addictions *diseases* fails to distinguish between thoughts and behaviors. While it may describe how people *think* when they value a substance or an activity over their own and others' well-being, it never explains how they behave, because *acting* on impulsive thoughts is virtually always voluntary. For example, there may very well be people who have hyperactive libidos and who, therefore, want to have more sex or more sex partners than most people do, but that's still no excuse for actually cheating on a significant other. And most importantly, calling a behavior a "disease" disempowers the individual to choose to change the behavior, which is ultimately the only cure that I know of for any addiction. I acknowledge that changing addictive behaviors is difficult, but it is not impossible. And as I see it, using words like *disease* and *relapse* simply serves up, on a proverbial silver platter, excuses for addicts *not* to work to change their ways instead of giving them the tools and courage they need to choose a better way.

EXTERNALIZATION VIA DISEASE

But addictions are far from the only bogus diseases used by celebrities and noncelebrities to externalize blame for bad behavior. Anger, rather than being an emotion that we're all expected to contain, is now considered a disease for which sufferers need treatment (never mind the suffering that these sufferers inflict on others!). Singer Justin Bieber was sent to anger-management classes as part of a plea bargain when he was charged with reckless driving and other offenses. Singer Chris Brown, famous for the horrendous battery of his fellow singer and then-girlfriend Rihanna, taking a page out of Tiger Woods' playbook, went a step further and checked himself in to a rehab facility for anger management.

Had I been the judge in either singer's case, I would've managed his anger with 100 percent effectiveness (at least in terms of preventing him from harming an innocent civilian anytime soon thereafter) by locking him up. And once the jail door slammed shut behind him, I imagine he would've somehow figured out how to manage his own anger almost instantly so as to avoid being educated in that skill by his fellow inmates (although that probably would've been faster and more effective treatment than what they got from my colleagues).

Sadly, addiction and anger (or, as it's sometimes clinically termed, "Intermittent Explosive Disorder") are actually two of the more plausible bogus diseases being used as externalizations of responsibility for behavior in America these days. For years, both on *Fatal Vows* and on various national news programs, I've analyzed cases in which women have murdered their husbands in cold blood—shot their husbands while they were sleeping, for example, or in one *Fatal Vows* story, hired someone else to kill the husband—and then claimed that the husbands had been abusive and that they (the wives) had become so paralyzed by fear that they could see no other way out of those abusive situations.

Domestic battery is all too real; when it happens, it's a very serious crime, and I'm glad to see some of our professional sports leagues—the NBA, NFL, and NASCAR—helping to amplify that message by taking stronger public stands against it. Again, better late than never. What's *not* real, however, is a mental disease—often dubbed "battered woman syndrome"—that deprives female (or any) victims of domestic battery of the ability to think rationally outside of the throes of any violence, identify alternative means of escaping those situations, and differentiate between right and wrong, legal and illegal, and so on.

Nevertheless, battered woman syndrome has been used time and again as a defense to murder charges. Sometimes it has worked, as it did for a New York woman, Barbara Sheehan, in 2011, who was acquitted of murder despite having shot her husband *eleven* times while he was . . . beating her or threatening to beat her? . . . no, shaving. Although she wasn't in any imminent danger when she pulled the triggers (yes, "triggers"—she used two different guns), she argued that, because of past abuse, she couldn't have been expected to figure out that she had any other option—like calling 911, fleeing the home, filing for divorce, and so forth. In that case, there was at least some evidence that the husband had been abusive in the past, but too often in such cases, there's been little or no documented history of any abuse whatsoever—no police reports, no witnesses, nothing other than the defendants' words, which the deceased husbands, of course, haven't been around to refute. While I hate domestic batterers, the remedy for that problem isn't allowing their partners to be their judges, juries, and executioners. But it gets worse!

You've probably heard of the infamous "Twinkie defense," a term coined during the 1979 trial of Dan White, who had killed San Francisco mayor George Moscone and city supervisor

Harvey Milk. In some ways, the term is a misnomer; Twinkies were never really mentioned by the defense in that case, nor was White's overconsumption of sweets ever really blamed for the killings. The defense argument was that White was depressed and, as such, his capacity to think rationally, though still present, had been diminished; thus, his degree of culpability for the killings was reduced. The overconsumption of sweets was used only as evidence of the depression, as White allegedly had been a healthy eater prior to the depression. And it worked, sort of. White was found guilty of voluntary manslaughter instead of murder. Since then, the term "Twinkie defense" has been generalized to encompass all assertions that a rare or unusual disorder absolves someone of responsibility for their criminal behavior. Enter, the "Anbesol defense" (better make that the "imbecile defense")!

One of the most unbelievable, and also one of the more tragic, cases that I've analyzed for the news networks was a 2009 case in which a New York woman (I can't bring myself to call her a "mother"), Diane Schuler, attempted to drive home intoxicated after a camping trip with her family. Loaded in her minivan were her son, daughter, and three nieces, all under the age of nine. Schuler drove the wrong way on a divided highway. The frightened nieces actually called their parents to say there was something wrong with Aunt Diane, and other drivers called the highway patrol to report the wrong-way driving, but authorities weren't able to get to her in time. Schuler crashed head-on into an oncoming vehicle, killing herself and everyone else in her minivan except for her son (who was critically injured) as well as three people in the other vehicle. Toxicology later found excessive concentrations of alcohol and marijuana in her bloodstream, with indications that both substances had been consumed either shortly before or even *during* that morning drive.

An attorney representing Schuler's husband (probably worried that the husband would be charged with child endangerment for allowing the children to ride with his drunk, drugged wife) argued it wasn't the alcohol and marijuana that had made Schuler drive so erratically—it was Anbesol, a topical anesthetic commonly used for toothache pain. Anbesol happens to be benzyl alcohol, not the same as the ethyl alcohol found in adult beverages. I actually took a few swigs of it on the air over the course of an hour-long program to demonstrate that it might be able to cause some slurred speech (due to numbness, although I didn't even experience that), but not intoxication. But even if, in theory, a person could get drunk on Anbesol, an adult would have to consume an absurd quantity of the stuff. Nevertheless, no charges were filed against the husband, who allegedly was a participant in the camping trip and had left the campsite in a different vehicle around the same time as his wife. Think that's the most bogus excuse for vehicular homicide you'll ever hear? Sorry, it gets worse.

In 2013 Ethan Couch, age sixteen, stole beer from a Texas Walmart, got drunk (toxicology later measured his blood alcohol content at approximately three times the legal limit for an of-age driver—there's no permissible quantity for an underage driver), drove his father's pickup truck approximately seventy miles per hour down a road that had a forty-mile-per-hour speed limit, swerved, killed four people on the side of the road at the scene of a broken-down vehicle, and seriously injured two additional people, one of whom became permanently and severely disabled. Couch was charged as a juvenile (in my opinion he should have been charged as an adult) and ultimately pled guilty to four counts of intoxication manslaughter and two counts of intoxication assault causing serious bodily injury; that's six felonies.

Enter perhaps one of my most profoundly misguided colleagues, a psychologist who proceeded to tell the sentencing judge that Couch deserved leniency. Why, you ask? Because he was drunk? No, the law generally doesn't (and neither should you!) allow people to voluntarily impair their judgment and then moan that their judgment was impaired—intoxicated or not, they're still expected to own their actions. So did the psychologist testify that Couch was *addicted* to alcohol and that his intoxication was therefore *not* voluntary? No, the testimony was even more ridiculous than that! The psychologist testified that Couch suffered from "affluenza," a nonexistent condition whereby an indulgent upbringing lacking in structure and discipline supposedly had diminished his capacity to know right from wrong. Never mind that surveillance video of the beer theft suggested otherwise; Couch apparently knew enough to conceal that theft, and any effort to conceal evidence or to evade detection or capture implies consciousness of guilt. It was psychology malpractice, in my opinion, but it worked. In a subsequent act of what, in my opinion, was judicial malpractice, the judge sentenced Couch only to probation (ten years) and a stint in rehab. Four human lives extinguished; no meaningful consequences. That's about as bad as it gets.

And as a psychologist with substantial forensic practice experience, I can assure you that even real and severe mental diseases are rarely—*extremely* rarely—enough to render one incapable of distinguishing right from wrong (by society's standards, which, practically speaking, means legal from illegal) and from self-restraining one's behavior to within the rule of law. And as was the case with addictions, it's critical here to separate thoughts from behaviors—criminal *impulses*, which may be involuntary products of diseases, from criminal *behaviors*, which virtually always are voluntary products of choices. For example, a pedophile may experience involuntary impulses to touch children sexually; those impulses are the essence of the disease of pedophilia. But the pedophile can resist acting on those impulses, just as we nonpedophiles can resist acting on our involuntary impulses to touch other adults sexually. So if the pedophile ever acts on any of those impulses, that's almost certainly a choice to violate the law. He has no "disease" defense; he's just guilty, period. And by the way, I believe it's impossible for me, or any psychologist, to ever talk a pedophile out of being attracted to children, just as it'd be impossible for a pedophile to talk me out of being attracted to adult women. So even if you think the pedophile might be "not guilty by reason of insanity," practically speaking, it doesn't much matter; there's still not likely to be a "safe" time to turn him loose among the public again. For example, a recently paroled pedophile once showed up at my office for a postrelease psychological evaluation driving his new "work" vehicle . . . an ice-cream truck. (Don't worry. When the judge found out, that particular ice-cream truck and its driver were off the streets very quickly.)

Even psychotic people (who usually aren't very dangerous, by the way; it's tough to premeditate much crime when one doesn't know which end is up or which planet one's on) who commit criminal acts can still be guilty, and they usually are. Eddie Ray Routh killed Chris Kyle, made famous by the movie *American*

Sniper, and another man, Chad Littlefield. Routh then pled not guilty by reason of insanity, purported to be psychotic (although his reported symptoms all sounded either greatly exaggerated or completely fake to me), was diagnosed as a paranoid schizophrenic by at least one psychiatrist, and was quoted as saying, "It [shooting Kyle] wasn't a want; it was a need." Routh also reportedly considered shooting Kyle and Littlefield while riding in Kyle's vehicle but decided to wait until they arrived at their destination, a target-shooting range, and apparently then to wait until Kyle's and Littlefield's guns were empty, so as to minimize his own chances of being injured while committing the murders. (Cowardice is a common thread among ambush murderers. They want to inflict pain on others without feeling any themselves; that's why school and shopping-mall shooters choose venues where they think nobody's likely to be armed, and it's why they tend to commit suicide or flee as soon as an armed person shows up.) Then after committing double homicide, Routh fled in Kyle's vehicle and led police on a high-speed chase. That's really all I needed to hear. If he was planning ahead, if he was making choices, if he was trying to evade capture, then, psychotic or not, he was capable of ascertaining that his actions were wrong. In other words, he's guilty, as his jury concluded.

The bottom line is that virtually everyone's capable of at least distinguishing right from wrong, and, except in rare instances of involuntary movement disorders or "tics," there's really no such thing as an *ir*-resistible impulse—there are only *un*-resisted impulses! And if someone's not resisting a resistible impulse, then you can generally assume that, to them, it's not worth resisting. In other words, what they're getting out of indulging the impulse is worth more to them than what they'd get out of resisting it. But "disease," both the fake and the real, isn't the only externalization of blame that's popular these days! Another favorite externalization of Americans these days is "a bad childhood."

EXTERNALIZATION VIA
UPBRINGING

As a psychologist I hear it all the time, though I hadn't heard it quite like this until I read a 2013 article by Akhil Sharma on Elle.com. The headline read, "Addicted to the Thrill of Sleeping with Married Women," and while that particular addiction doesn't exist, what was even more appalling than how he externalized adultery to a bogus disease was how he externalized the origin of it: When Akhil was ten years old, his fourteen-year-old brother dove into a shallow swimming pool and became profoundly disabled, after which the brother's care consumed the majority of their parents' attention. The overwhelmed parents, particularly the mother, became irritable and short-tempered with one another and with Akhil. Then, when Akhil was fifteen years old, a forty-something married woman, who had befriended the family and offered social support in the time since the brother's accident, seduced Akhil, beginning the first of a series of sexual relationships between him and married women, which he went on to recount in the article. While I felt sorry for Akhil in the sense that he allegedly was a statutory-rape victim, what struck me even more was the overarching theme of his article, which was that his subsequent, completely volitional adulterous behavior as a man was mostly everybody's fault but his own.

Now, might Akhil's parents, overwhelmed by the needs of his disabled brother, have neglected Akhil's needs, such that he developed a narcissistic character rooted in self-pity? Sure. Might Ethan Couch's parents have indulged their son excessively and unconditionally such that he developed a narcissistic character rooted in self-aggrandizement? Absolutely (I wish I could put them *and* their son in jail!). But here again, the experiences of pedophiles are illustrative. They often *have* suffered sexual abuse as children themselves, which is heartbreaking and may have something to do with how they developed their pedophilic impulses, but it's still no excuse for acting on such impulses. And when people use such childhood experiences as excuses, it's insulting to everyone who had similar childhood experiences yet went on to be upstanding, law-abiding Americans (which, thankfully, is most of them). At some point, we have to expect everyone who has the capacity to differentiate right from wrong to do so and to self-regulate their behavior accordingly. Sure, that's easier for people who had good upbringings, but as is the case with genetic vulnerabilities to over-eating and other addictions, just because something's harder for some of us than others doesn't mean we can't all be expected to do it. To put it bluntly, if we allowed adults to go around crapping on others just because their potty training wasn't good, we'd be mired in a lot of unnecessary crap.

DEFLECTION

If we don't tolerate externalization—that is, if we don't let people moan about supposed external causes of their behavior when it results in some kind of harm to themselves or others—does that mean they'll necessarily own the behavior? Unfortunately, no. Often, they'll attempt deflection; they'll attempt to shift the focus of attention away from *their* behavior by pointing instead to the behavior of *others*. Sometimes they'll deflect because they're wallowing in denial of their own faults—for instance, because it's painful (humiliating, despairing, etc.) for them to admit, even to themselves, that they've caused harm, so they're desperate to identify someone to share, if not *bear*, the blame. Freud referred to that as a form of *projection*, whereby people subconsciously try to keep their self-esteem intact by identifying their own faults in others instead of in themselves. And sometimes people deflect precisely *because* they're acutely aware that they've caused harm, so they're anxious to divert criticism from bad behavior of theirs to worse behavior of others.

In 2014, after Dean McDermott, husband of reality TV star Tori Spelling, was caught cheating on Spelling, it came as no surprise—at least not to this host of a show about marriages gone spectacularly wrong—that McDermott's public statements included expressions of regret. Did he regret that he had cheated? Not so much. He claimed he might *not* have cheated if Spelling had paid more attention to him! Virtually every wrongdoer I've ever assessed as a psychologist has tried to spend more time talking with me about other people's faults than their own. And just think about how often, in your own daily life, or as you read or watch the news, you hear people claim that they're not doing as well as they could be or should be because of white people, or black people, or rich people, or poor people, or men, or women, or the police, or "corporate America," or various historical grievances, or people from other countries. . . . How often are such blanket deflections really valid in this day and age in America? Virtually never! They generally serve only to absolve the deflectors of accountability for their circumstances and to excuse them from doing anything to improve those circumstances (more on this topic in Chapter 6).

The most dumbfounding deflection in recent memory comes courtesy of a couple of deadbeat debtors from Florida. (And here's another instance where colleagues of mine—this time in the legal profession—have contributed to the problem.) In 2009 a married couple apparently fell behind in their mortgage payments to Bank of America. Understandably, a debt-collection subsidiary of the bank then started trying to reach the couple by telephone, but they didn't cooperate. So, instead of simply initiating foreclosure proceedings (as I would've done after about the second call!), the bank's representatives made approximately 700 attempts to reach the couple over a four-year period. Then in 2014, what did the husband and wife do? Bring their mortgage payments up to date? No, apparently not. Apologize for borrowing money they couldn't afford to repay and for being uncooperative with the bank? No. Hand the house keys over to the bank? No, apparently not that, either. They *sued* Bank of America, alleging that the bank had subjected them to "patterns of outrageous, abusive, and harassing conduct." Incredibly, they won, over a million dollars. They borrowed the money, didn't pay it back on time, and didn't cooperate with the lender. Then, instead of owning their irresponsibility, they hired a lawyer who moaned on their behalf that the couple were victims. What's worse, we—American society—helped in this case, via a legal system gone way too soft. (Is it any wonder that banks have become more conservative about mortgage lending in this environment?)

So if externalization doesn't work, and if deflection doesn't work either, at that point, are Americans forced to own accountability for their behavior? If only! No, there's another powerful tool in the sociopath's toolbox that many everyday Americans have become highly skilled at using: minimization. Sometimes they minimize by "normalizing" bad behavior (e.g., "Everybody's human"). Sometimes they minimize by rationalizing bad behavior (e.g., "It made sense under the circumstances"). Sometimes, they minimize by emphasizing the *effect* of bad behavior over its *intent* (e.g., "No harm, no foul"). And sometimes they minimize by simply dismissing bad behavior altogether, as if no bad intent was involved (e.g., "It was just a mistake").

MINIMIZATION VIA NORMALIZATION

Normalization is really just another twist on Freud's concept of projection. By focusing on identifying faults in others, one first attempts to avoid admitting, even to oneself, that one harbors those same faults. But if self-incriminating evidence builds to a point where it's no longer deniable, one can then fall back to the position that the characteristics are not really faults, because "everyone" has or does them; they're "normal." And normalization isn't used only to excuse individuals' bad behavior; it's also used to excuse bad behavior occurring within sizable subsets of entire populations.

"Defining deviancy down" is an expression credited to the late U.S. senator Daniel Patrick Moynihan, used in reference to what I call "pseudo-solving" societal problems by simply explaining them away as "normal." For example, if there's a problem with teenagers "sexting," we can either try to find solutions to that problem, or we can pseudo-solve it by simply declaring it normal for teens to act out sexually using electronic media. Voila, problem solved!

MINIMIZATION VIA RATIONALIZATION

Then there's rationalization. In early 2015 I appeared on Dr. Drew Pinsky's radio program to discuss some interesting new statistics on marital infidelity. Given all of the disastrous consequences of cheating on one's spouse, one might reasonably expect that the average IQs of cheating spouses would be lower than the average IQs of faithful spouses, but I had found a statistic that in fact suggested the opposite—that cheating spouses' average IQ was higher than faithful spouses' average IQ. The difference was so slight that it probably wasn't statistically meaningful, but I explained that it actually *was* consistent with something I've often said about intelligence: It's an asset in almost every other area of life, but the one place where it's a liability is in the rationalization of bad behavior in which an intelligent person wishes to engage.

When I'm called upon to assess, counsel, or coach executive-level businesspeople (such as physicians in hospitals) whose behavior has damaged the reputations of or disrupted their organizations, I'm still amazed at times by how convoluted their rationalizations are and yet how they're able to make serious breaches of professionalism or ethics sound almost understandable under the circumstances. As I told Dr. Drew, a highly intelligent person can almost rationalize the irrational. And my social-scientist colleagues have created an entire body of literature that *actually helps* intelligent people rationalize degeneracy.

I recall one guy in particular—highly intelligent, financially successful, high profile in his field—who was ordered to see me for an evaluation after getting himself in some serious legal trouble stemming from his efforts to conceal expenditures of money on an extramarital affair. It was fascinating, in a reprehensible sort of way, to listen to this guy regurgitate one line of amoral drivel after another from supposed research articles in support of his contentions that "humans aren't built to be monogamous" and that "America would be better off if we were more like European societies when it comes to the acceptance of extramarital relationships." He was well-read and eloquent enough to almost make one wonder whether he was onto something—until I asked him, "If you weren't built to be monogamous, and you don't think promises of monogamy are honorable, then why did you promise someone monogamy?" He had no answer, but had he been honest, the answer of course would have been that, back when he made that promise to his wife, he wanted something, namely her hand in marriage, so he made the promise to benefit him*self*, not her, and once he got what he wanted, he no longer felt the need to give up what he had promised to give up in exchange for it: other women.

MINIMIZATION VIA EMPHASIZING EFFECT OVER INTENT

Perhaps the best example in recent memory of minimization by emphasizing the effect over the intent of behavior occurred in the context of what came to be known as "Deflategate." In early

2015, as the New England Patriots were gearing up to play in Super Bowl XLIL, it came to light that some footballs, provided by the Patriots and used in the playoff game that had secured the Patriots' Super Bowl berth, had been partially deflated, ostensibly making them easier for the Patriots' quarterback, Tom Brady, to throw. The NFL investigated; scientists weighed in on whether there could've been a benign meteorological explanation for the deflation, and the media reported on it as if it were a scandal of Watergate-like import. It was the stuff of publicists' dreams! And as a psychology/law/culture pundit, I probably would have stayed out of it had some of my sports-pundit colleagues not opined (paraphrasing multiple individuals), "The Patriots won that playoff game so decisively that they clearly would have won it whether they cheated or not, so it's no big deal—no harm, no foul." But it was a big deal, in this sense, which few pundits mentioned: We may think we know what would have happened if the Patriots had *not* cheated (and maybe they didn't), but we really cannot know for sure what would have happened if the *opposing* team *had* cheated, whether by deflating its own footballs or by some other means. If any cheating is tolerated, whether that particular cheating ultimately affects the outcome of a game or not, then there's always harm, to the team that played by the rules and didn't do as well as it might have had it cheated also. And even if the cheating didn't ultimately affect the outcome of the game, intent still matters; a person who tries to do something wrong shouldn't be excused simply because they didn't succeed. They should be punished just as they would be if they had succeeded.

MINIMIZATION VIA DISMISSAL

Finally, there's minimization by dismissal, the most common, most annoying dismissal of all: "I made a mistake." How many public figures can you recall getting caught cheating on their wives and then, often through crocodile tears, pleading for their wives' and the public's forgiveness using such mockingly minimizing words to dismiss deliberately destructive behavior? President Clinton did it. Tiger Woods did, too. So did Jim Bakker. You yourself may have been on the receiving end of the "mistake" minimization sometime in your life, and if so, (a) I'm sorry for you, and (b) I hope you didn't buy it! A "mistake" is an *accident*. When one misspells a word, for example, that's a mistake. When one intends what occurs, as when one cheats on one's spouse, that's never a mere "mistake." Whenever an offender uses that minimization with me, I always ask, "What part of your behavior was unintentional?" and they never have an answer. I understand why they like to use the word "mistake"; it's morally neutral, but that's precisely what makes it inappropriate.

THE POWER OF ACCOUNTABILITY

It's understandable why people moan about being held accountable for their behavior. Nobody likes being accountable. It's often emotionally, financially, and otherwise painful. But there's empowerment in accountability. In many cases, true accountability can go a long way toward repairing damaged relationships, and even when it can't, it at least can empower one to chart a new and better behavioral course for oneself. Are there ever times when we're really not responsible for our behavior, or lack thereof, and an excuse really is legitimate? Yes, but those times tend to be relatively few, and even in such an instance, if we really want to avoid a reoccurrence, we usually have more power to change our own behavior than to change the external world, the behavior of others, the past, and so on. So, if we truly want to behave in healthier, more productive ways in the future, we need to stop moaning about accountability and start owning it!

Yet just as we have many Americans continuing to moan about their lack of happiness, and continuing to moan about their lack of things, we have many Americans continuing to moan about accountability. If moaning's ultimately so ineffective, why do so many of us continue moaning instead of owning, and what will it take to change? I'll tell you coming up in Part II.

PART II:

THE AGE OF ENTITLEMENT

CHAPTER 4

Why We Moan

Neurotics complain of their illness,
but they make the most of it, and when it comes
to taking it away from them they will defend
it like a lioness her young.

—Sigmund Freud

THE ENTITLEMENT EPIDEMIC

Part 1 of this book focused on what Americans today are moaning about. I devoted a chapter to each of three major "moans" that I—and probably you, too—have been hearing all too frequently in recent years. Part II of this book is about *why* there seems to be so much moaning in a nation where, generally and relatively speaking, people are so richly blessed. I've spent my career thus far explaining all manner of unproductive behavior and trying to help people do and be better. If a behavior's unproductive, chances are I've studied it, taught about it, consulted on it, testified about it in court, and covered it on national television for years. If you like trying to figure out why people do the unproductive things that they do, you've come to the right place. And moaning, for the most part, is profoundly unproductive!

So why are we doing it? Why are we moaning when we're not as happy as we want to be instead of owning our ability to make ourselves happy? Why are we moaning when we don't get things that we need and want right away instead of owning the ability (which the vast majority of us have) to fulfill our needs and wants through productivity and patience? And why are we moaning when we've behaved badly instead of owning accountability for our behavior by apologizing and making appropriate amends? The answer, in a word, is *entitlement*. We've become increasingly self-focused and self-entitled, in part because of our basic human nature, in part because we haven't been raised and educated to be otherwise, in part because our culture has progressively promoted it, and in part because our civil society hasn't imposed enough negative consequences for it.

Entitlement is the common thread tying together the societal problems that I've been talking about on national television for the better part of a decade now. On the relatively minor end of the spectrum, there are increasingly frequent discourtesies, like talking loudly on cell phones in restaurants, leaving shopping carts to roll around into other shoppers' cars in grocery store parking lots, cutting in front of other people in traffic, and other innumerable transgressions that would make Miss Manners shriek. Then there are varied forms of more serious irresponsibility, like overeating and overburdening the healthcare system with preventable cases of heart disease and diabetes, overborrowing and overburdening the financial system with underwater mortgages, rampantly abusing the latest designer intoxicants along with medical marijuana, and applying for public assistance when many applicants could survive without it. Then at the extreme end of the spectrum, there are mass murders in our schools and other public places, committed by people who've gratified their warped desires or soothed their hurt feelings at the expense of others' very lives.

An entitled self-indulgence connects all of it, and its destructive marks are visible at every level of our society—from insufferable individuals to messed-up marriages, failing families, bankrupt businesses, communities in crisis, and a nation in need of renewal in order to stay ahead of our (mostly figuratively but somewhat literally) "leaner and meaner" global competitors in the years ahead. Too many people no longer see themselves as parts of something larger than themselves and no longer have compunction about using, abusing, or endangering their fellow Americans for short-term gratification. Collectively speaking, we've experienced a cultural drift, kind of like the continental drift that we learned about in high school science class. These drifts happen so gradually that we don't often notice them until there's a major negative scientific event like an earthquake or a volcanic eruption, or a societal event such as a mass shooting. So how do people come by the entitled attitudes that cause such problems at the personal, interpersonal, organizational, economic, and societal levels?

NARCISSISTS BY NATURE?

Actually, an entitled attitude comes naturally. Each of us enters the world about as narrowly focused on our own needs as we could possibly be. It's not that we didn't *care* that our moaning for bottles and diaper changes kept our parents awake night after night; as infants, we didn't realize that our parents even continued to exist when they weren't in the same room with us! We had no sense at that developmental stage of being part of anything larger than ourselves or of having any obligations to be or do anything for anyone else. Nor should we have at that stage. We were completely incapable of fulfilling our own needs; those who brought us into the world really did owe us our living. So the question is less about how we *get* self-focused and more about why so many of us *stay* so self-focused even as we grow in our abilities both to fulfill our own needs and to understand the needs of others.

Throughout our lives, that same basic instinct that caused us to moan for our parents' attention when we were uncomfortable as infants remains with us, and we share it with the entire animal kingdom. It's the drive to survive. Pain and discomfort, such as hunger, thirst, or excessive heat or cold, imply an existential threat, while comfort and pleasure imply existential safety. And as we grow into our reproductive years, for most of us, our drive to survive grows beyond self-preservation to include self-propagation, or procreation, so that something of us survives beyond ourselves.

Think of some things that people strive to attain in life: money, power, attractiveness, popularity. They all facilitate survival in some way. Money and power provide security against threats and unfulfilled needs while affording us access to excess—opportunities to fulfill many of our wants. Attractiveness and fame draw others to us and maximize our self-propagation chances and options; money and power don't hurt in that regard either—these things are often interconnected.

But as we grow into mentally and physically healthy adults, many of us come to realize that we're not the only ones trying to survive in this world, that *our* needs and wants aren't the only needs and wants that matter, and that there are at least practical advantages both to fulfilling our needs and wants independently and to helping others to fulfill their needs and wants. Many—but not all—of us come to those realizations. And whether we do or don't has a lot to do with our parents and other educators and how well they prepare us to navigate a popular culture that has progressively reinforced—even codified—entitlement. In other words, it all starts at home.

NURTURING NARCISSISM

No matter how well-meaning, parents tend to be the foremost nurturers of narcissism, the personality trait from which entitlement grows. Freud suggested that parents literally spoil their children's personalities when they "are under a compulsion to ascribe every perfection to the child—which sober observation would find no occasion to do." In 2015 a study conducted by researchers at The Ohio State University[19] essentially affirmed Freud's sober observation, finding parents' overvaluation of their children (e.g., constantly telling the children that they're the prettiest and smartest and most talented and all-around best children in the world) to be the single strongest predictor of whether children will develop narcissism. In that same study, children who had been overvalued were significantly more likely to endorse statements such as, "Kids like me deserve something extra," beautifully illustrating how narcissism translates into entitlement.

Many American parents today don't just overindulge their children with *praise*; they also overindulge their children with *things*. When parents go beyond satisfying all of their children's needs and start satisfying all of the children's wants as well, they literally spoil the kids' chances of learning how to manage resources responsibly. When kids learn to expect excess rather than to anticipate scarcity, they learn to expect needs and wants to be satisfied equally rather than to differentiate and prioritize between and among them. They also learn to expect others to make sacrifices for them rather than to be self-reliant. They lose the connection between getting what they want and doing something of value, and they learn to go about getting what they want by using others rather than by making themselves useful to others. They also learn to expect instant gratification rather than to delay gratification, a tendency that separates achievers from nonachievers in every society that I've observed in my travels to thirty-five countries on seven continents. Whether you go to faraway bustling cities like Bangkok, Thailand, or Alexandria, Egypt; to small towns in the Peruvian or Chilean Andes; or to islands in the Caribbean or the Pacific, you'll see, as I have, that those who invest the time to develop marketable skills and then work hard to produce quality goods and services for others tend to enjoy a better quality of life than those who, despite being able-bodied and -minded, succumb to the short-term allures of laziness, intoxication, crime, and so on.

Persisting differences between individuals' tendencies to forgo relatively small, immediate rewards in favor of larger, delayed rewards have been attributed to various genetic and environmental factors, the most powerful of which, I believe, is parenting—parental expectations as well as parental examples. A foundational study of delayed gratification conducted in the 1950s (even before Walter Mischel's famous marshmallow studies[20]) found that the single strongest predictor of kids' failures to delay gratification was the absence of two parents—the absence of fathers, specifically—from those kids' homes. This conclusion should give pause to anyone who's inclined to think that the absence of *things* from kids' homes explains certain "cycles" of poor decision making (e.g., less saving and more spending, particularly on things of fleeting value, such as fast food and entertainment, and things that may feel good in the short term but are destructive in the long term, such as cigarettes and drugs) that we see all too often among those least able to afford to waste money.

By the most recent estimates, over one-third of American children and adolescents are overweight, and approximately one-fifth are obese; a child who is obese in the single-digit ages is highly likely to struggle with weight throughout adulthood.[21] Obesity is now a pediatric health epidemic, and the short- and long-term consequences for America's young people are literally heartbreaking. Physically, concerns include heart disease, diabetes, sleep apnea, and a host of other problems. Psychologically, concerns include poor self-image, generalized impulse-regulation problems, social exclusion (even ridicule—it's not right, but it happens, and it hurts), and other relational problems (e.g., difficulty finding dating partners and spouses). For these reasons, I say that an obese child is an abused child. Parents are largely in control of what their children eat, at least prior to mid-to-late adolescence, which makes parents primarily responsible for childhood obesity. It's not about what foods children want; it's about what foods children need, which means that parents are responsible for procuring and apportioning what kids eat. Even when it comes time to reward kids for jobs that truly *are* well done, parents should be careful about using food as the reward. In moderation, it's probably fine, but kids' attitudes toward food, like other core values and life skills, tend to be internalized early and remain stable over time, so parents should encourage them to think of food primarily to meet physiological rather than psychological needs.

But many American parents today don't just overindulge their children with praise and with things. They overindulge their children behaviorally as well, imposing precious few expectations and limitations upon their children's behavior. For example, to prevent childhood obesity, in addition to regulating which foods are available to kids and in what quantities, parents also need to regulate the amount of sedentary time their kids spend on social media, video games, TV, and so on, so that it's balanced with healthy periods of physical activity. It never ceases to amaze me, though, how reluctant many parents are to say "no" to their kids.

THE NEED FOR "NO"

In 2013 actress Marla Sokoloff made news when she announced that she was cutting the word "no" out of her parenting vocabulary as much as possible. In a TV interview, Sokoloff said, "I just felt like that evil mom who was just always reprimanding my child, and I hated myself and my parenting skills" (honestly, I don't love her parenting skills either, which is why I wouldn't recommend taking parenting advice from the *Desperate Housewives*, of which Sokoloff was one). Sokoloff also said that prior to her epiphany about the word "no," her daughter (who looked to be all of about three years old) had heard it so often, "It got to the point where she was literally laughing in my face." I don't know what your household was like growing up, but in my household, when Mom told us "no," no matter how often, nobody was laughing in her face. So here again, one has to question parenting advice from an adult who admittedly has had a hard time getting a toddler to take her seriously!

Then in 2014 actor Will Smith's thirteen-year-old daughter made news when a somewhat-concerning photo of her and a shirtless twenty-year-old male actor appeared online. One published report about that incident[22] contained the following quotes from Mr. Smith: "We don't do punishment"; "The way that we deal with our kids is, they are responsible for their lives. Our concept is, as young as possible, give them as much control over their lives as possible . . . and the concept of punishment, our experience has been it has a little too much of a negative quality"; and "You can do anything you want as long as you can explain to me why that was the right thing to do for your life." What? If you're contemplating becoming a parent, and you don't want to "do punishment" because you're too lazy, or you think it's too "negative," please, just don't become a parent—because if you do become a parent, you must "do punishment" in order to help your child(ren) learn to avoid repeating destructive behavior. Any "parent" who lets a thirteen-year-old do whatever she wants as long as she thinks it's "the right thing to do" for her life gets an F in parenting from me.

In that same vein, over my years of covering crime on TV, I've discussed numerous cases involving "sexting"—people, often minors, sending sexually explicit images of themselves to one another using mobile devices or social media. And time after time, the most stunning aspects of those cases to me, beyond the stupidity of those doing the sexting, have been the reactions of their parents. I've heard parent after parent haplessly moaning, saying things like, "What can I do? Kids'll be kids," as if they, the parents, hadn't, in the vast majority of cases, *paid* for the devices; as if they hadn't *paid* for the bandwidth; as if they hadn't both the right and the *responsibility* as parents (and this is true whether they paid for the devices and bandwidth or not) to *monitor* their minors' behavior in cyberspace; as if they hadn't the responsibility to do whatever they could to *prevent* their minors from engaging in behavior that could damage them, seriously and irreparably— and could lead to even *more* damaging behavior. Kids who are overindulged, technologically and behaviorally, by overpermissive parents, and who then become sexually active in cyberspace, are likely to become sexually active in the physical world sooner than they otherwise might, exposing themselves (no pun intended) to myriad potential hazards that they're ill-prepared to navigate (STDs, pregnancy, emotional distress, and so on).

Are today's American parents *trying* to ruin their kids and, in the long run, their culture? No, I don't think so. I just think many parents are profoundly misguided. They don't realize that the child who's allowed to do whatever he or she wants, or to take whatever he or she wants from them (the parents) today—because they think the child is so cute or because they're preoccupied or they're feeling guilty or they're just weak—are setting the stage for disaster. Such children will likely turn into the adolescent, and ultimately the adult, who expects to do whatever he or she wants, and to take whatever he or she wants from people, often resulting in devastating consequences. The eight-year-old who talks back to his parents with no consequences and hits his sibling because he's mad that she made a face at him, again with no consequences, is more likely to be the eighteen-year-old who drinks underage at college, drives while intoxicated, hits someone with his car, and then is genuinely shocked when the jail door slams behind him.

Many American parents today are starting out with the wrong idea of what it even means to *be* a parent. This job is the most important and often most demanding one that a person will ever have, as well as the most rewarding in the long run. The goal is to get one's child to the age of majority as physically, intellectually, emotionally, and morally healthy as possible. That means fulfilling the child's *needs*; it does not necessarily mean fulfilling the child's *wants*. In fact, it means *denying* the child's wants if, in the parents' best judgment, fulfilling those wants isn't in the child's long-term best interests. In practice, that means denying a lot of wants—saying "no" a lot of times—over the course of eighteen years and bearing the moaning of the child, whose mind isn't mature enough yet to make the best decisions. This is precisely why the child needs the parent and why we make a distinction in our laws between minors and adults. Will Smith's minor kids aren't "responsible for their lives," not yet—he and their mother are. Unfortunately, many American parents have abdicated their parental responsibilities to teach kids to differentiate wants from needs and to make healthy decisions about whether and how to fulfill them. Instead, they've overindulged their kids in myriad ways and for myriad reasons.

Affluence—or, as I've termed it, "access to excess"—has played a role, but that's really just a tradeoff of one problem for another. Less affluent parents who lack the resources to fulfill their children's material wants often also lack the resources to provide their children with certain material "extras" (e.g., voice-to-text software so that kids can write papers by simply speaking into their computers instead of typing) that can help their children become as productive as they could be, academically and occupationally. More affluent parents have less trouble providing *those* kinds of extras, but they need to worry more about providing too many extras, sapping their kids' motivation to be as productive as they could be. Overindulgence, though, whether in praise or the material overindulgence associated with affluence, is just one path to narcissistic entitlement. Just as overindulged kids can end up with a narcissistic entitlement rooted in aggrandizement (first parental aggrandizement, then self-aggrandizement), kids whose needs, whether for affection or for material things, are neglected can end up with narcissistic entitlement born of anger, resentment, and jealousy.

Across the spectrum of affluence, one of the most common reasons for parental overindulgence is guilt—for not being home enough, for getting divorced, and so on. I wrote about guilt in Chapter 1, specifically about how the productive function of guilt is to prompt a change in the behavior that produces the guilt (e.g., the absenteeism, the divorcing) and, if possible, to prompt amends making for the harm that the behavior has caused. Soothing one's own conscience at further expense to the harmed party is not making productive use of guilt; it's actually compounding the original harm. But perhaps the most common reason why parents overindulge their kids is a subconscious, though nevertheless fundamentally selfish, desire simply to feel the kids' affection—to be liked by their kids. Actress Marla Sokoloff said that part of the reason she wanted to stop telling her daughter "no" was that, "I think she was starting not to like me." Then, after she adopted her no-"no" parenting policy, Sokoloff said, "I felt better about my*self* as a mom" (emphasis added).

But it's not about how parents feel about themselves or what parents want from kids; it's about what kids need from parents. The current and immediate past generations of American parents seem to have decided that the parenting style of the Greatest Generation (the WWII generation) is passé—that structure and discipline, even when administered lovingly, are simply too confining, too stressful for kids. Today's parents have largely abandoned those tried-and-true, time-tested parenting principles, and in a short few decades, we've seen American parents morph from the Greatest Generation into what might accurately be described as the Weakest Generation. Many parents today are trying way too hard to be their kids' friends and not nearly hard enough to be their kids' parents, the results of which can be devastating for all concerned. Yet once children start behaving in narcissistically entitled ways, rather than holding the children accountable, today's parents are the first to make excuses for the children's behavior.

Remember those adults back in Chapter 3 who externalized responsibility for their bad behavior by blaming it on their bad childhoods? They actually have a point, in this sense: While their parents generally are not responsible for their (adult children's) bad behavior, the parents may very well be responsible for teaching them to externalize blame. Many parents model externalization in their households while their children are growing up, and many parents practice externalization on behalf of their children until the children are old enough to practice it for themselves. In yet another profound break from the parenting style of the Greatest Generation of American parents, who emphasized both accountability and self-reliance in problem-solving, today's so-called "helicopter" parents are all too eager to swoop down on their children's schools, activity venues, and places of employment (all the way up to and including their adult children's workplaces) to rescue their children from their own irresponsibility, and when those "helicopters" land to pick up their kids, they usually also want to drop off a load of . . . externalization. (What did you think I was going to say?)

MEDICATING VS. DEDICATING

And when it comes to externalization via disorders and conditions, it's amazing how many responsibility-absolving diagnoses of kids I see today, compared both to past generations of Americans and to my colleagues' experiences in other countries: behavior disorder diagnoses in cases of kids who are just brats, nonspecific autism-spectrum diagnoses in cases of kids who are just behind in social-skills development, vague thyroid-dysregulation diagnoses

in cases of kids who are just fat, and on and on and on. Of all of
the responsibility-absolving pediatric mental health diagnoses, by
far the most-often bogus, most overhyped, overdiagnosed, over-
medicated, and generally overblown is Attention Deficit Disorder
(ADD, or with hyperactivity, ADHD). By the most recent estimates, over 10 percent of American kids ages four to seventeen,
approximately 6.4 million kids, have ADD/ADHD diagnoses.[23]

**Percentage of American Kids Ages 4–17
with ADD/ADHD Diagnosis**

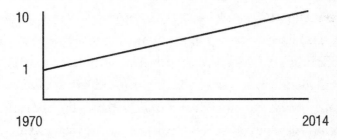

What's more, a majority of those kids are taking prescription
medications for their supposed attention deficits, medications
with potentially serious physiological and psychological side
effects. Physiological concerns include heart problems, appetite
and growth suppression, and insomnia. Psychological concerns
include dependence, psychosis, mood changes, and stifled indi-
viduality and creativity, not to mention what it does to a kid to
simply tell that kid, "There's something wrong with your brain,
and you need to take medication for it." Not great for the kid's
self-image, but a great excuse for the kid not working to improve
attention and behavior self-regulation. In addition, prescription

ADD/ADHD medications are being rampantly diverted on high school and college campuses, most often for recreational use, exposing even more kids to criminal, addiction, and overdose risks. Not surprisingly, these drugs are turning up more frequently in the American workplace as well.

Funny thing: Nobody seems to have had ADD or ADHD back when the Greatest Generation parents were parenting. Even today, far fewer people seem to have it, relatively speaking, in a lot of other countries than in the United States.[24] So is that because we healthcare professionals are just so much better now at identifying disorders here in America while our colleagues in other countries lag far behind? Not unless we consider countries like France and Australia to "lag far behind"; those countries have state-of-the-art health care yet relatively low frequencies of ADD/ADHD diagnoses. Perhaps French and Australian clinicians understand that the biological basis for these diagnoses is still very poorly established. We still can't point to exactly which part of the brain supposedly is malfunctioning to cause the reported symptoms on which American clinicians—often pediatricians with little training in differential mental health diagnosis—base their diagnoses. The truth is, if a kid can sit and watch a movie or play a video game for hours, then the kid can focus attention. So it's probably not a matter of ability to focus attention and sit still; it's probably a matter of motivation to do so.

Perhaps French and Australian parents are culturally more reluctant than Americans to externalize blame for their kids' behavior. If so, I think it reflects a sort of double externalization whereby American parents absolve both their kids and themselves of responsibility for the kids' bad behavior. Parents in America today also seem all too willing to opt for the quick fix of a pill when there are behavioral interventions that can be equally— even more—effective but require remedial increases in parental involvement and effort. They require, as I often say, "dedicating rather than medicating." In any case, the epidemic frequency of these diagnoses in the United States is largely an American phenomenon. I seriously doubt that 10 percent of American kids could have the same mental disorder; this is statistically too high to be credible. If so, then we should rename this disorder: ADD could stand for American Discipline Deficit, and ADHD could stand for American Discipline and Humility Deficit.

And just as millions of American parents are externalizing their kids' bad behavior and poor academic performance to ADD/ADHD, millions more are externalizing their kids' delayed social skills development to various other often-amorphous diagnoses along the autism spectrum. While there certainly are kids whose obvious and debilitating deficits fall at the severe end of that spectrum and warrant intensive clinical intervention, many others have purported deficits that are barely, if at all, detectable and don't warrant any diagnosis on the autism spectrum, let alone clinical intervention. The latter group of kids are within what we call the "normal" spectrum, often just not as far toward the high end of that spectrum as their parents would like. So once again, instead of accepting that those kids might be late bloomers, instead of accepting that those kids might even be—God forbid!—average, instead of looking to just make sure they're doing everything they can to foster those kids' healthy, if not advanced, development, parents go looking for diagnoses.

If you doubt me, consider that in 2000, the Centers for Disease Control estimated that one in 10,000 American kids had an autism diagnosis. By 2005, diagnoses had increased over tenfold to one in 1,000. Then a few years later, it was one in 150, then one in 110, then one in eighty-eight, and most recently, one in fifty. At that rate, pretty soon, it'll be one in two, and we'll have to start calling it "normal" to have an autism-spectrum diagnosis. Unless much of humanity has always been semiautistic and we diagnosticians are finally getting good (exponentially better by the month!) at spotting it, either this is one of the fastest-spreading epidemics in human history (that's what some advocacy groups would like you to believe, releasing study after study linking autism to everything from vaccines to plastic baby bottles to paternal age at conception to . . .), or there's a major externalization factor in play. I believe, of course, that the latter is the case, and it's frightening because many kids with autism-spectrum diagnoses are being prescribed trials of psychiatric medications that are far more powerful and of which the short- and long-term side effects are far less predictable (because they've been neither formulated for nor extensively tested in children) than ADD/ADHD medications.

NOT *MY* KID!

Parents these days aren't just doing a lot of externalizing on behalf of their children. They're also doing, and teaching their kids, a lot of deflection. Coming back to my many discussions of sexting cases on TV, I've been additionally stunned to hear parent after parent, mothers and fathers alike, moan more about school officials, law enforcement, prosecutors, and so on—about the adults who ultimately did those parents' jobs and intervened to stop the behavior—than about themselves for failing to supervise their kids or about the kids for engaging in the behavior (more in Chapter 5). It's a stark illustration of just how much parenting in America has changed for the worse. When I was a kid, if I had gotten in trouble with school officials or the law, I would've been in *more* trouble at home (and I think the same was true for most of my friends). It's frightening how that has changed, particularly now that a combination of affluence and technology has afforded many millions of immature minds, focused as they are on short-term gratification, the means to do irreversible long-term reputational harm to themselves and to one another, not to mention put themselves in the way of the life-threatening harm that lurks in the depths of cyberspace (e.g., pedophiles, child pornographers, human traffickers, rapists, . . .).

Yet parents today are even deflecting blame for their children's behavior in courts of law. In 2011 a mother appeared on Dr. Drew Pinsky's TV show after her fifteen-year-old son died of alcohol poisoning. Whom did she blame for the son's death? The son, for behaving so recklessly? No, even though he apparently had committed two crimes, one in obtaining the beverage and a second in consuming it. Herself, for not having supervised the son better? No, even though she apparently had driven him to, and dropped him off at, the concert where the lethal drinking took place. The convenience store from which the son had illegally obtained the beverage? No, although that would have made some sense. She blamed the company that produced the alcoholic beverage that the son drank, and she was suing that company. See what I mean? As sorry as I felt for her, and as much as I would've admired her

had she simply come on the show and told her story as a caution-
ary tale for other parents, I mostly just ended up feeling appalled
at how focused she was on finding someone else to blame for the
son's—and her own—behavior (which, sadly, may have somewhat
explained the origins of the son's irresponsibility).

Today's parents also frequently practice, and teach kids, the
art of minimization. How many times have you heard a parent of
an overweight child minimize the problem by saying something
like, "Oh, she's just big-boned like her father"? Parents who have
their own weight problems, in particular, are more likely to minimize their kids' weight problems, which is why all parents need to
consult their kids' pediatricians about healthy weights and diets.

NOT *ME!*

And sometimes, here again, parents minimize kids' weight
problems because they simply don't want to do the hard parenting work that it would take to get the problem under control. A
thin mother with a thin husband, one thin child, and one obese
child once asked me, "What am I supposed to do? Change the
whole family's diet?" Clearly displeased by my, "Yes, ma'am,
that's correct," response, she didn't change a damned thing, and
she now has one thin adult child and one obese adult child who's
likely to encounter problems physically, if not emotionally and
socially, for decades to come. Whatever else she was doing back
then instead of parenting couldn't possibly have been worth that.

There's a paradox worth noting here: with respect to obesity,
parents are normalizing pathological behavior; sedentary couch-
potato kids parked in front of electronic screens munching on

junk food when they should be outside moving around. At the same time, with respect to ADHD, they're pathologizing normal behavior—highly active kids who seem hyperactive by comparison. Might this paradox help explain why we have millions of obese kids as well as millions of kids on ADHD medication in America today? I think so.

In terms of parental models of minimization, I've been literally nauseated on multiple occasions when adolescent girls whose fathers have abandoned their families to take up with affair partners have parroted their dad's minimizations to me: "My dad made a mistake." While I realize it's easier for them to think that way than to accept the truth—that 50 percent of their genes came from a morally bankrupt individual—I worry about how that kind of thinking is going to manifest itself in their own relationships down the line: mistrust of honest suitors, trust of dishonest suitors, tolerance of infidelity, or even infidelity of their own. In my professional opinion as a child custody expert, it's emotional child abuse for a parent to hurt and confuse a child that way.

NO CHILD LEFT ACCOUNTABLE

The nurturance of narcissism starts at home, but it doesn't stop there. Too often in America these days, this nurturance continues in our public schools. For the past thirty-plus years, K–12 educators have placed a profound overemphasis on self-esteem. It began innocently enough, as a means of countering the self-dissatisfaction that led, and still leads, to phenomena like depression and eating disorders among young people. But when misguided educators (and parents), well-intentioned as they may be, promote unconditional self-esteem; when schools cancel honors ceremonies and relax standards so that no child has to feel the unhappiness of not measuring up academically; when scores aren't kept or when coaches are punished for winning too decisively so that no child has to feel the unhappiness of not measuring up athletically; when we're all expected to pretend like national holidays and traditions don't exist so that no child has to feel the unhappiness of not participating in those holidays and traditions, what do we end up with? We end up with American kids who conclude not only that their happiness is paramount but that they're actually entitled to have happiness handed to them by others.

Parents who actually are modeling and attempting to nurture healthy levels of accountability at home unfortunately aren't getting a lot of help these days from their children's schools. In 2008 I wrote a column for WorldNetDaily titled "No Child Left Accountable," in which I detailed efforts in public school districts across America to reduce academic accountability. For example, in Grand Rapids, Michigan, F grades had been banned. Instead, when a student's work was insufficient to pass a course, the teacher was required to assign a placeholder grade of H, which stood for "Held," and to allow the student three months to complete alternative work online. Meanwhile, in Boston, there was a new policy called "ZAP" ("Zeros Aren't Permitted"), whereby failing students were given time during the school day to go back and complete work that they hadn't completed satisfactorily on time. And in Dallas, homework deadlines had been banned, teachers were required to drop their students' lowest homework scores, and students were being allowed to take every test multiple times and keep their best scores. Proponents of so-called no-failure measures said they'd encourage fewer dropouts, but in reality, they had simply defined deviancy down. There may be a student or two here and there who has made productive use of these measures over the intervening years, but it's likely that far more have seen the measures as a license for failure, which does nothing but reinforce underachievement and send young Americans into the adult world unprepared, set up to fail, and expecting to be rescued. Here again, our global competitors love to see us sabotaging ourselves this way because the results will be less globally competitive Americans.

It's not just academic accountability that's being abandoned in our nation's K–12 public schools—it's *behavioral* accountability, too. Schools across the country are replacing traditional disciplinary policies, whereby offenders were kept after school, suspended, and so on, with "restorative justice" programs, whereby consequences involve offenders (including those who've committed crimes like battery and theft on campus) sitting down face-to-face with victims and listening to how their actions made their victims feel. In many school districts, students can't even be suspended for cursing at teachers anymore. And suppose we really can restore the status quo ante (that's legalese for "the way things were beforehand") after an offense—for example, if a student steals another student's cell phone, and we catch the thief, and we make him return the phone—that's not justice.

In order for there to be justice, the victim needs to see that the community (the school or the broader community, via the police and criminal justice system) takes the violation of their rights seriously and imposes a punishment on the offender. There also needs to be a deterrent to future violations of people's rights by the offender. If the phone thief gets caught today and all he has to do is return the stolen phone, there really isn't much of a reason for him not to try stealing another phone tomorrow. And above all, if there's to be any valid expectation that the phone thief will go on to be a productive American rather than escalating in his antisocial behavior, someone needs to try to impress upon him that stealing is wrong, but in today's world of litigious helicopter parents, getting tough to find a public school educator willing to recommend that a student actually follow one of the Ten Commandments.

CAUTION: NO-VALUES ZONE

I'd like to tell you that K–12 schools are the only places where educators are misguidedly fueling entitlement in America today, but it's happening at colleges and universities, too. I think that college professors, many of whom are "religiously" secular and relativistic in their thinking, have redefined "intelligence" for many young Americans as the mere ability to understand both sides of an argument with no need to discern which side is correct. The typical American college campus (and textbook) thus has become a no-values zone, where all sides of an issue share equivalent value and the search for mere understanding has replaced the search for truth. Many college professors in the social sciences have become rock stars in the eyes of their students, not because they say anything truly intelligent, but because they're moral contrarians. Terrorists and American soldiers—functional equivalents. Marital fidelity and infidelity—equally valid choices. Child pornography and religious symbols—equivalent forms of expression.

Increasing college completion rates among Americans are good—they contribute to increased productivity for Americans and for America as a whole—but as that has happened, too many pseudointellectual college graduates, misguided by pseudointellectual professors, have gone on and tried to live value-neutral lives, which simply doesn't work very well. Remember the fairytale, "The Emperor's New Clothes"? In it, con artists posing as tailors defraud the emperor by selling him clothes that they claim are visible only to intelligent people. Rather than admit that he can't see the clothes, the emperor ends up walking naked through the streets of his empire and becomes a laughingstock. There's important adult wisdom to be gained from this simple children's story because some of the emperor's tailors have earned PhDs and have embarked on new careers as college professors.

HOME, SCHOOL, AND CHURCH VS. POPULAR CULTURE

If you think about where a young American historically would have acquired values that counter narcissism and entitlement—such as empathy and respect for others and a sense of duty to behave in *pro*social rather than antisocial ways—three key venues should come to mind.

- **First**, there's the home, but as we've seen, it's not happening there like it used to. Due to rampant divorce and materialism (i.e., the pursuit of second incomes for lifestyle reasons even when families could live comfortably on one income), fewer parents are present in young Americans' homes these days to model and teach such values, and the parents who are present are often too busy, too exhausted, too wrapped up in their own narcissistic pursuits, or too guilt-ridden to spend much time instilling functional values in their children. And many parents who *are* present and who do devote the time to instill functional values in their children nevertheless often overvalue, overindulge, and overpermit while absolving their children of accountability.

- **Second**, there's the school, but as we've seen, it's not happening there like it used to either. There's a misguided emphasis on self-esteem, not enough emphasis on academic or behavioral accountability, and virtually no emphasis on instilling or reinforcing functional values for fear of upsetting parents who don't share those values.
- **Third**, there's the church (or synagogue, or other place of worship where functional values routinely are discussed and promoted), but here again, it's not happening there like it used to because fewer American families than ever are attending regular religious services.

So, if functional values haven't been instilled or reinforced in young Americans at home, school, or church, it's no wonder they are remaining relatively self-focused well beyond early childhood. That's a bigger problem today than ever before in our nation's history, because when they leave their homes and schools, Americans enter a culture that not only condones but promotes narcissism and entitlement at every turn.

Social media promotes constant comparisons of users' lives to other users' lives—all of which tend to be selectively portrayed, if not outright exaggerated, to appear happier and more affluent. Entertainment, from popular music to movies to reality television to professional sports, increasingly celebrates people who self-indulge in profoundly irresponsible and destructive ways. Ubiquitous advertising promotes constant envy of others (again, often idealized others whose bodies, possessions, and experiences set impossibly high standards), encourages the immediate indulgence of one's every material whim, and offers quick fixes or escapes from one's every problem (e.g., pills for everything from happiness to weight loss without any dietary or lifestyle changes). And even after the Great Recession (2007–2009), relatively lax barriers to obtaining credit enable Americans to overindulge in the short term rather than delaying material and experiential gratification until they can comfortably afford it. While credit can be a good thing, both for individual borrowers and for the overall economy —most Americans, for example, couldn't purchase homes if they had to pay cash up front—there's a difference between using credit to acquire things of lasting or appreciating value like homes and using it to acquire things of fleeting or depreciating value like meals out and entertainment. Americans are doing far too much of the latter, both individually and collectively.

In short, today's American culture emphasizes quick and quantity over gradual and quality and has gone a long way toward eradicating the shame associated with overindulgence in any form. All of this sends the message to Americans, young and not-so-young, that the world revolves around them, that if a thing makes them feel better about themselves, they deserve to have it, and that their immediate wants, rather than either their own long-term best interests or the impacts of their actions upon others, should drive their decisions. Thus, over the past fifty years, American culture has progressively reinforced excessive self-focus and self-indulgence (narcissism) and the attitude that life is mostly about getting what one "deserves"—in other words, entitlement.

THE NEW SECULAR CLERGY

I'm embarrassed to acknowledge that some of my fellow mental health professionals have been willing participants in that effort. While many Americans have abused alcohol and illicit substances to escape mentally from negative emotions, far too many others, like Anna Nicole Smith, have obtained similarly short-term chemical escapes from psychiatrists and from other medical doctors and nurse practitioners playing psychiatrists. But perhaps even more insidious, many psychotherapists have actively assisted Americans in concocting rationalizations to facilitate entitlement and resultant destructive behavior. While well-intentioned, when the overarching goal of therapy is each patient's happiness, therapists tend to identify all negative emotions like anxiety, guilt, and shame as impediments to happiness, which are to be eliminated regardless of their origins. It's a phenomenon about which I've been speaking and writing for years: Americans turning to mental health professionals for guidance on how to live their lives. And it's no surprise. With fewer and fewer Americans internalizing strong systems of functional values at home, school, or church, millions of Americans in search of answers to life's dilemmas have been looking to psychotherapists almost as a new breed of secular clergy.

Here's the big problem with that approach: The typical American psychotherapist's office is likely to be a temple of relativism,

or as I've often called it, "if-it-*feels*-right-it-*is*-right-ism." I titled a
2013 column on this topic for WorldNetDaily, "Forgive Me, Doctor, for I Have Sinned . . . ," and continued into the column's open-
ing lines, ". . . sayeth the patient. Then sayeth the doctor, 'Fear
not, my patient. If it felt right to you at the time, then it was right.
Now go, and feel guilty no more.'" Silly as it may sound, similar
dialogues occur daily in psychotherapists' offices across America.
As I explained in my column, many people who are motivated
to become mental health professionals tend to believe, a priori,
that human behavior is shaped largely by forces beyond our control, even beyond our awareness. As psychotherapists, then, they
tend to be secular humanists, whose well-intentioned, overarching (and misguided) goal is each individual patient's happiness.
Thus, they tend to convey unconditional positive regard for their
patients, no matter how destructive the patients' behavior, and to
conceptualize their patients' negative emotions as impediments
to happiness that must be eradicated, no matter how rational,
informative, and constructive those emotions may in fact be. In
my professional experience, the typical American therapist simply
is neither well-trained nor inclined to teach patients to use negative emotions productively.

I'm not suggesting that Americans shouldn't see psychotherapists for help with symptoms of mental illness, or for objective,
supportive sounding boards during stressful times, or for subject matter expertise on effective strategies to deal with interpersonal problems. I am suggesting that Americans shouldn't rely
on the typical psychotherapist for solutions to problems that are,
in essence, moral rather than clinical. In my experience, it is a
rare psychotherapist who's both inclined and equipped to help

patients complete the concerted intellectual, interpersonal, intro-spective, and spiritual work involved in establishing a framework of values upon which to build purposeful, productive lives. Thus, psychotherapy tends not to be the effective shortcut around that work that many Americans seem to be seeking.

A case in point: A few years ago, I read a column from a writer who had pursued an extramarital affair and had ultimately aban-doned a faithful spouse and children to be with the affair partner. The column referred to a therapist as having been the "shaman" or "spiritual guide" who had helped the author find the "cour-age" to pursue "happiness" via the affair, notwithstanding the destruction that it wrought upon the family. More recently, I read a column by a woman who had been in a sexual relationship with a single father and had developed an attachment to his young child before deciding to break it off with the father in order to pursue happiness as a single mother via artificial insemination. The woman described having asked her therapist for advice on whether and how to "break up" with the man's two-year-old child and was counseled that it was "folly" to put the child's happiness above the author's own happiness. See what I mean? Two people smart enough to write published articles ended up rationalizing their treatment of human children as if they were pets in the furtherance of their happiness.

Those people's counselors would have served them much better had they not facilitated their escapes from negative emotions but rather helped them explore the origins of those negative emo-tions. I recall a therapy session I conducted several years ago in which a teenage patient disclosed to me that she had been smok-ing marijuana with friends on weekends. I asked her whether she knew about the potential effects of drugs on her body and mind and how her drug use might affect her relationships with her parents and peers, her reputation and legal record, her current and future education, her current and future employment, and so on. Eventually, she covered her ears and yelled at me, "Stop it! You're making me feel bad!"

I replied, "It's about time." Sadly, her aversion to hearing the truth and changing her behavior accordingly illustrated what happens to kids when adults model the pursuit of happiness over goodness, of feeling good over being good, examples of which abound.

EXCUSES ANYONE?

At the same time, people who claim to have behavioral expertise are selling accountability-absolving products for everything from weight loss to improved academic performance in all manner of media all across America. I often see a TV commercial for a diet plan that includes a testimonial from a woman who exclaims, "You just can't do it on your own, you can't!" (Yes, you can, more often than not, regulate how many calories you consume and how much you move without paying a dime to anybody else for assistance.) Then there's an annoying radio commercial for a product called something like "The Easy Way to Get an A." "Failing grades don't come from bad or lazy kids!" claims the narrator (yes, they do, more often than not), they come from kids who are *bored* in school, because they're smart but unstimulated. Well, if nothing else, he (or whoever wrote his script) knows how to sell a product to today's American parent by essentially saying, "Your kid's not lazy or dumb! He's actually gifted! Your genes are great! So is your parenting! Neither you nor your kid needs to do much (other than buy this product) to get his teachers to finally see his giftedness, too!"

Too many mental health professionals are all too happy to sit in their offices (and worse, in court!) and dole out those responsibility-absolving diagnoses like sex addiction, so that a guy like Tiger Woods can come off better in a child-custody battle; or ADD, so that a student who gets bored in Shakespearean literature lectures can get extra test-taking time at school to "accommodate" that "disability" (a student with an ADD diagnosis can even get extra time on the test for admission to medical school now; how would you like to have *that* doctor on duty if you ever need to go to the ER?); or agoraphobia, so that an extremely shy adult can stay at home and collect Social Security disability income instead of overcoming shyness and working; or even affluenza, so that a punk like Ethan Couch can go free after killing four people.

But it's not just mental and behavioral health professionals; there's a whole guilt- and fault-absolving industry, made up also of lawyers, the media, pharmaceutical companies . . . modern-day merchants of absolution (what the medieval church once called "indulgences"). For example, in 2008 I heard a radio commercial for a firm seeking clients with debt problems, which started out like this: "Bankruptcy—it can happen to anyone, at any time, and it's probably not your fault!" No, bankruptcy can't happen to "anyone"—one first has to borrow more money than one can pay back. And no, bankruptcy typically can't happen "at any time"—one typically takes a while to accumulate the kind of unrepayable debt that results in bankruptcy. And yes, if one *is* bankrupt, it probably *is* their fault—who else's fault would it be?

Meanwhile, as fast as addiction researchers can produce an endless parade of accountability-absolving *studies*, the media eagerly publicizes them because today's American audiences tune in to accountability-absolving *stories* such as, "Why You Just Can't Put Down the Crisps" (also known as "chips" in American English; notice the word "can't" instead of "won't"), and "Oreos Just as Addictive as Drugs, Study Finds," or even "Justin Bieber's Arrest: Addicted to Wealth and Power?" There have been so many of them that, in recent years, I've participated in a fairly steady series of segments debunking them on Fox News Channel's daytime program *Happening Now*. Part of the problem is, as I explained to my lawyer colleagues in a 2014 journal article,[25] nobody pursues a career in the study of addiction if they don't subscribe to the conceptualization that it's a "disease," and once one enters that field, their professional livelihood depends on grants, studies, and publications that corroborate that very conceptualization.

At the same time, the pharmaceutical industry spends billions of dollars ubiquitously pushing the notion that every behavioral problem is a "chemical imbalance," that nothing's anybody's fault, and that they have a pill (or a liquid, or an injection, or a spray, or an inhalant . . .) for everything from obesity (no exercise or diet moderation required!) to alcoholism, to your kids' rambunctious behavior, to adult pop singers' anger outbursts. Mix up some of my mental health colleagues (plus general practitioners and pediatricians practicing outside the scopes of their expertise), with all of those drugs, with an American public looking for externalizations and quick fixes (for themselves and for their kids), and you've got one powerfully dangerous cocktail with not nearly enough accountability in it.

A big part of why we're hearing so many excuses for not owning in America today is that Americans have become all too accepting of these phenomena. In other words, a big part of why we moan is because it works! Given how little time Americans are devoting to the discussion of values in their homes, public schools, and religious congregations, it's really no surprise that we've developed a pervasive cultural reluctance to make value judgments about one another's behavior. Culturally, we've made a virtue of being nonjudgmental. We've convinced ourselves that there's something wrong with (1) calling out the bad behavior of others and (2) ostracizing those who behave badly. It has been the single greatest victory of narcissistically entitled hedonists (people who believe in if-it-*feels*-good-it-*is*-good-ism) in the history of humanity, and there are multiple reasons for it, the first of which is a fundamental misunderstanding of what it means to be judgmental.

WHO ARE *YOU* TO JUDGE?

It's probably the biggest criticism I've received over my years in the national media: "You're too judgmental!" Sometimes it's phrased as a question, "Who are you to judge?" And sometimes it's even accompanied by scriptural quotes (which I suspect are some of the only such quotes that some of my critics have memorized), like, "Let he who is without sin cast the first stone," or "Judge not lest you be judged." Those people have conflated judgment of one's salvation-worthiness—where one belongs in the hereafter, which I agree is no job for a mere mortal like me— with judgment of the quality of one's behavior in the here and now. Is the behavior productive or destructive? If it's destructive, particularly to others, it doesn't mean we need to stone anybody (certainly not for an offense like extramarital sex, which is what the scriptural stone-throwing incident referenced above was about), but it doesn't seem logical to me, nor am I aware of any religion that says that unless our own behavior has been perfect throughout our lives, we must not recognize destructive behavior for what it is and must acquiesce to its repetition.

There's also, I believe, a pervasive misunderstanding of forgiveness in our society today. While I often hear that I need to be less judgmental, I also often hear that I need to be more "forgiving" (sometimes with an accompanying "Turn the other cheek" scriptural reference). I'm all for forgiveness, but not for the benefit of the perpetrators of destructive behavior. In my view, forgiveness is primarily for the benefit of victims of destructive behavior. It enables them to let go of rage and the desire for vengeance and get on with their lives. Forgiveness doesn't mean that the perpetrators of destructive behavior shouldn't have to pay any consequences or that their victims (and would-be victims) should have to put themselves back in harm's way so that the perpetrators can have second (or third, fourth, fifth, . . .) chances to inflict harm. And even if you believe in forgiveness for the benefit of the perpetrators of destructive behavior, forgiveness isn't likely to be transformative, even for them, unless it's granted in response to genuine remorse and appropriate amends-making.

Multiple mistresses of Tiger Woods have given interviews in which they've claimed to be "sorry" for helping Woods hurt his family. They're not sorry. If helping a married man hurt his family really bothered these women, they wouldn't have done it. Of course, the same applies to every philandering male public figure who has stood in front of television cameras in recent years telling us how ashamed they've been for having let down their families, constituents, fans, and others. If they really felt that cheating on one's wife was shameful behavior, they wouldn't have done it. I don't see a lot of genuine, appropriate shame in American culture these days, yet I see Americans being quite loose with their forgiveness, doling it out in response to the most insincere, emptiest of apologies. For example, after Lance Armstrong (the professional cyclist who accepted numerous accolades and millions of dollars in sponsorship and prize money over years of competitions in which he cheated by doping) went on television and gave—no, not the millions back—a tepid apology to Oprah Winfrey, many of the students in my college course that semester said they'd be in favor of lifting Armstrong's ban from professional cycling, just because he articulated an apology. All was forgiven, no apparent sincerity, no apparent amends—no wonder so many people cheat!

Why are Americans so quick to accept empty apologies and lame excuses and to forgive bad behavior these days? Three key reasons:

1. Some genuinely believe they're being virtuous and altruistic.
2. Others are simply scared to acknowledge that there's evil in the world. They'd rather think that the perpetrators of destructive behavior all have something clinically wrong with them. I know it might be more comforting if everyone who did bad things to others had an illness, because then maybe someday psychology and psychiatry could prevent most if not all destructive behavior by curing those illnesses. Well, we won't. Take it from me, there are

evil people in the world, and you don't have to be religious for that term to have meaning to you. I'm not using the word in a religious way either. Yes, my colleagues have come up with a diagnosis for them, too: "Antisocial Personality Disorder," psychology's way of getting around having to label them "bad." But semantics aside, that's basically what they are: bad people—malignant narcissists who feel entitled to take what they're not owed regardless of whom they hurt in the process (more on them, and the essence of evil, coming up in Chapter 5).

3. Some Americans are reluctant to find fault in others' behavior and are quick to accept excuses and forgive fault if and when they do find it because they are driven by their own narcissistic entitlement. They don't want to judge others' behavior, even when it's destructive, lest their own behavior be judged by others, so they're quick to excuse and forgive with the expectation that they'll quickly be excused and forgiven if and when the time comes.

ENTITLED BY LAW

Finally, we've actually codified, and in doing so, reinforced a culturally pervasive sense of entitlement via "progressive" (i.e., evolving in step with our culture) public policy. Propagandizing terms like "inequality" and "greed" in our political discourse in recent years has further distorted Americans' concepts of what's fair and of what they feel they deserve from others in life, falsely implying that those who have less are somehow entitled to share in what belongs to those who have more. And in a democracy where a majority of citizens who have less can vote to redistribute among themselves what belongs to a minority of citizens who have more, that ought to trouble all of us—morally (because it's wrong), economically (because it always ends up shrinking economies rather than growing them), and historically (because it has never, in the entire history of the world, strengthened a nation long term).

Now, if the inequality rhetoric in America centered on ways to encourage and enable those who have relatively little (materially speaking) to produce more, that would be one thing. Instead, though, the focus more often seems to be on characterizing those who have relatively much (again, materially speaking) as greedy. Like envy and jealousy, greed is another often-misunderstood concept. As I see it, greed is willingness to acquire things through destructive means—to defraud, steal, or extort—for example, to knowingly sell a product with a hidden defect that could maim or kill a buyer (even in the "Robin Hood" story, it's implied that the "greedy" rich people's wealth is ill-gotten, thereby "justifying" the hero in ambushing and stealing from rich people like a literal "robbin' hood"!). But the mere desire to acquire things, through legitimate means, and the assertion of a right to self-determine whether and how to share one's legitimately acquired things with others are not "greedy."

We're not helping matters by continually referring to our public assistance programs as "entitlements." When we do that, we're reinforcing the expectation that millions of Americans are "entitled" to have goods and services purchased for them by other Americans. In essence, we're teaching people to transition from moaning to their parents to moaning to the government, when, in fact, the last thing any of us should want is a government that treats us like its children (more on that in Chapter 6). Yet over 100 million Americans have embraced that entitlement mentality in some form. I remember driving several years ago listening to the radio when a commercial came on featuring a grandmother who spoke about how she was raising her rambunctious grandchildren and how they were running all over her neighborhood doing all kinds of fun physical activities all the time. I thought that it was going to be a commercial for Geritol or maybe Depends, but no. Her next line was, "That's where food stamps come in," and she went on to explain how she used the government's Supplemental Nutrition Assistance Program (food stamps) to make sure that her grandchildren got the nutrition that they needed. I couldn't believe that we, as a nation, had actually started advertising, essentially recruiting recipients, for public assistance, but we had. By 2014, roughly one-sixth of Americans were signed up for food stamps. I think it happened more because of entitlement attitudes than advertising, but the advertising certainly reinforced the attitudes.

We haven't just codified entitled expectations; we've also codified nonjudgment. For example, we'll hand out food stamps even if the reason someone can't afford food is that they're lying around doing drugs all day long.

An even more egregious example in my view is so-called no-fault divorce, a legislative triumph of nonjudgment. Once upon a time in America, if a husband cheated on his wife, not only would most people in their community have branded him a jerk and a loser, but she could also have divorced him and left him relatively penniless. Over the past couple of decades, though, there has been a legislative preference for efficiency over justice in divorce litigation, whereby most judges no longer even try to sort out which spouses actually broke their marriage contracts, let alone to then penalize those spouses in their divorce decrees. Not only is a cheating husband now considered ethically fit to be president, but thanks to no-fault divorce laws on the books across America, he can walk away from the marriage with half of the marital assets and half of the custodial time with any minor children (and in most jurisdictions, that amoral process still isn't very efficient!). Guess what happened to divorce rates in America as these laws became commonplace? They skyrocketed.

Traditionally, the marriage contract was secular society's way of supporting, sanctioning, and encouraging the kind of long-term, committed, monogamous relationships in which manageable numbers of children would be produced, provided for, and co-parented by mother-father teams. It was a contract not to be entered into lightly, because in it, society took an affirmative interest in maintaining a couple's commitment to one another. Today, when we give a marriage contract less force than a gym membership contract, it's really no wonder that so many people view marriages as disposable. In terms of teaching young Americans functional values, just *imagine* the disillusioning message that it sends to a twelve-year-old girl when her father cheats on her mother, precipitates a divorce, moves in with his affair partner, expects the daughter to spend half her time at his house being respectful to the affair partner—which, in my professional opinion, is child abuse—yet the law says there's no fault in his behavior.

SLAP . . . SLAP . . . SLAP . . .

It's bad enough that we're codifying the acceptance of nonjudgment in our civil law, but it gets physically dangerous when we do it in our criminal law. Remember Eldo Kim from back in Chapter 1, the Harvard student who made a bomb threat to postpone taking a final exam for which he wasn't prepared? Well, guess what happened to him? He got the federal equivalent of diversion—deferred prosecution—the conditions of which included a few months of home detention, some community service, and some restitution for the costs of the law-enforcement response (i.e., the search of the premises where Kim had claimed explosives were located). In other words, next to nothing happened. Surprised? Sadly, I wasn't. I've been involved in the coverage of most of the major criminal cases you've seen on national television for the better part of the last decade, and in the majority of those cases, the perpetrators have received this same sort of catch-and-release treatment on multiple prior occasions before their destructive behavior escalated to whatever it was that finally captured national attention.

You've seen the likes of Lindsay Lohan, Chris Brown, and Justin Bieber get slap on the wrist after slap on the wrist, and you may have thought that the problem was preferential treatment for wealthy celebrities. No, the problem is that the same thing is happening all across the country, day in and day out, to defendants who are neither wealthy nor famous. As of 2014, one-quarter of those arrested for, and almost one-third of those convicted of, driving under the influence (of drugs or alcohol, "DUI") in the United States were found to be repeat offenders.[26] So does that mean they're going to jail, where they can't endanger you and me on our roads again for significant periods of time? Hardly. For instance, in early 2015 in my home state of Kansas, not generally considered a soft-on-crime state, a man was sentenced to just three days in jail, followed by six months of "house arrest," for his tenth DUI conviction. The maximum available sentence was a year in jail, which *still* would've been far too lenient, in my opinion.

And as I was writing this chapter, an apparent panhandler was arrested about a block from my residence for stabbing a seven-teen-year-old boy in the neck after the boy declined to give the panhandler money. No surprise: the panhandler has four prior battery convictions—and he's only twenty-five years old! Just imagine how little time, if any, he must've served for those prior four convictions, combined, in order to be back out on the street and under arrest—again—all by the age of twenty-five (and keep in mind, those are just his priors that we know about). So is the local prosecutor throwing the book at him this time, charging him with attempted murder? No, the charge is battery—again—only this time with an "aggravated" in front of it. So is the local judge at least going to keep the defendant locked up until his trial? No, bail was set at $15,000, meaning that as soon as the defendant (or some relative with misguided compassion for the defendant) can come up with just 10 percent of that, $1,500, he'll be right back out on the street—again.

As of 2009, approximately 75 percent of those arrested for fel-onies in the seventy-five largest U.S. counties had multiple prior arrests. Half of them had more than five prior arrests, and over one-third of them had more than ten prior arrests. Approximately 60 percent of those arrested for felonies had at least one prior conviction, 43 percent had at least one prior felony conviction, and 13 percent had at least one prior violent felony conviction. Thirty percent had multiple prior felony convictions, and 11 percent had five or more prior felony convictions. And these numbers have been on the rise.[27] Remember this next time someone tries to tell you that we're incarcerating too many people for too many years in the United States.

We accept excuse after excuse—Lindsay Lohan has an addiction, Chris Brown and Justin Bieber have anger management problems, Eldo Kim has test anxiety, etc. and we give people chance after chance, as if we're more concerned about the perpetrators of destructive behavior than about their past and future victims. It's really no wonder, then, that our streets are littered with people who behave destructively, who have no interest in changing their destructive behavior, and whose destructive behavior tends to escalate. Our failure to hold them accountable reinforces their entitlement while leaving them not only available but also unafraid to behave in progressively destructive ways among us. (And that's how we got a national violent crime rate that, in 2011, began rising for the first time in two decades.)

There you have them—the key reasons why so many Americans are moaning so much these days. The good news, though, is that people can and do transition from moaning to owning, under the right conditions.

CHAPTER 5

When We Own

> The fault, dear Brutus, is not in our stars,
> but in ourselves.
>
> —Shakespeare, *Julius Caesar*

THE ESSENCE OF OWNING

Up to now, this book has been all about moaning. We've examined the "big three" forms of moaning that are prevalent in American culture today: moaning about unhappiness, moaning about unfulfilled material wants, and moaning about accountability for behavior. We've explored why we moan, ultimately tracing the origins of moaning in all its forms to self-centeredness and self-entitlement. And before we even embarked upon this literary adventure, the book's very title,

Stop Moaning, Start Owning! foreshadowed the conclusion that moaning is bad and we ought to be owning instead.

What does it mean to "own"? For the purposes of this book, to "own" means to assume personal responsibility—for our happiness, for the fulfillment of our material needs and wants, and for our behavior—in this life rather than projecting that responsibility outward. To own is to realize that changing our lives for the better generally begins with changing ourselves.

But if moaning's in our animal nature, at least early in our lives, and it's reinforced by parents and schools and popular culture and even public policy, then how can we possibly be expected to stop moaning and start owning? Well, human beings are at once animals and something inherently, uniquely, wonderfully more. In addition to that drive to survive on a physical and genetic level, which we share with the rest of the animal kingdom and which accounts for much of our behavior, including our moaning, we humans have the unique capacity also to develop a drive to survive on an immortal level.

ABOVE AND BEYOND

This latter drive is not rooted in physical gratification, self-preservation, or even propagation of our genes. Instead, it's rooted in a powerfully motivating opportunity that only we humans can recognize—to achieve an existence on a metaphysical level, completely independent of our physical natures, which can take multiple forms. For many, it takes the form of an afterlife of some kind—an opportunity for our consciousness, our souls, to continue living beyond the death of our physical bodies. And

for many, in addition or instead, it takes the form of some enduring impression or legacy: the opportunity to make an indelible
mark on the world through something we've created, something
we've said, or something we've done. Doing so immortalizes us,
to some degree, by allowing us to continue to exist indefinitely in
the consciousness of others after we're physically gone. Recognizing the possibility of achieving immortality, in whichever form(s),
motivates us then to think about how our actions in this life affect
both the likelihood that we'll continue to exist afterward and, if
we do, the quality of that existence.

As Freud observed, our drives to survive on mortal and immortal levels often conflict with one another, and when that happens
throughout history, it has been considered admirable if one's drive
to survive on an immortal level wins out. Fortunately, not only are
we humans capable of recognizing such eternal survival opportunities, but we're also capable of prioritizing our pursuits of them over
and above even our mortal survival. Hence, humans are routinely
willing to die defending principles or to die defending others (who
aren't even genetically related) or to sacrifice their physical health
to complete works of art or literature, build businesses, and so on.
It's why, for instance, U.S. Army Pfc. Ross McGinnis would throw
himself on top of a grenade to save four of his fellow soldiers in
Iraq in 2006 (in 2008 McGinnis was awarded, posthumously, the
Congressional Medal of Honor for his valor); it's why Mozart
would race death to complete his masterpiece *Requiem* (and as
time ran out, left detailed instructions for how his protégé was to
finish it); and it's why Steve Jobs would continue working on Apple
products even as pancreatic cancer took a terrible physical toll on
him (Jobs reportedly worked until the day before he died).

HUMANKIND'S SAVING GRACE

So what is it that enables us humans to recognize opportunities to survive on an immortal level, prompts us to search for
ways to merit that immortal survival, and ultimately compels us
to stop moaning and start owning our destinies in this life and
beyond? It's our intellect, our ability to reason, to assess not just
how to continue existing in the mortal sense but why we exist in
the first place, and not just ourselves as individuals but all of us
as a human race. We can then evaluate which behaviors advance
the fulfillment of our purpose and which behaviors hinder it—
i.e., which behaviors are right and which are wrong. In short, we
stop moaning and start owning when we *think*. But to think or
not to think is our choice; it's the fundamental act of free will.
When we choose not to think and to base our behavior solely on
physiology or emotion—what *we* want in the short run without
considering others or the long run—we essentially reject our own
individual humanity and the humanity of others. We choose to
behave less like humans and more like animals, which facilitates
destructive behavior and moaning. Conversely, when we choose
to contemplate the impact of our actions upon others and to
behave in constructive ways, we embrace humanity, which facilitates constructive behavior and owning.

Although not everyone *does* think, everyone *can* think. I
believe that humans' intellectual ability to differentiate constructive from destructive behavior—right from wrong—is innate and
that it's not necessarily strongly correlated with cognitive development. For example, I've psychologically assessed adults with
cognitive disabilities and preteenage children who've been able to

articulate, at least rudimentarily, why it's wrong to steal other people's property. I've also psychologically assessed physicians with genius-level IQs who've used their high intelligence to rationalize and mastermind heinous crimes ranging from the distribution of narcotics to attempted murder. Therefore, when I've assessed someone who truly hasn't seemed capable of differentiating right from wrong, I've explained it as being less about the absence of an intellect and more about various kinds of barriers that have existed between the intellect and the outside world.

In order to make accurate differentiations between right and wrong, the intellect needs to have accurate information from the outside world, but some individuals' brains, due to neurological underdevelopment or dysfunction (e.g., mental illness or sensory impairment), aren't able to receive, process, and transmit the necessary information sufficiently. I liken it to trying to drive a car in which all of the clear glass had been replaced with thick stained glass; no matter how intelligent and how good a driver you were, you'd probably still run into things simply because of how difficult it would be to get accurate information about the environment in which you were driving. Fortunately, such individuals are relatively rare. As illustrated by my assessments of kids and cognitively disabled adults, the threshold capacity to make meaningful differentiations between right and wrong isn't very high. Most of the time, when people don't think, it's not an inability; it's a choice.

YOU KNEW IT ALL ALONG

A 2013 brain-imaging study of adults diagnosed with Narcissistic Personality Disorder[28] found atypically low levels of activity in the areas of their brains where empathy is processed, and some media outlets reported on that study as if it proved that self-entitled individuals—moaners—are physiologically incapable of accurately contemplating themselves in a broader human context, contemplating the impacts of their actions upon others, and adjusting their behavior accordingly. I explained back then that another way to interpret the study was far more plausible in my opinion—that rather than representing a genetic or developmental deficit in their brain tissue, the lack of empathic activity in the brains of narcissists represented atrophy, or degradation of brain tissue from nonuse. In other words, rather than being a *cause* of narcissism, the deficit observed in the study was more likely a *result* of narcissism.

Similarly, studies of psychopaths—whose core personality trait, once again, is narcissism, from which flows a sense of entitlement to gratify themselves by making others suffer—have found certain abnormalities in the areas of their brains where empathy and inhibition are processed. But here again, these findings imply no causal direction. In other words, they don't imply that people are born with neuro-developmental deficits that cause them to feel less empathy, have higher risk tolerances, and so on. Such findings may simply reflect how elective engagement in destructive behavior and taking progressively larger risks over time cause certain parts of the brain to atrophy. Regardless, I'm absolutely convinced that nobody is forced by neuroanatomy to consciously behave in destructive ways. Basic choices between constructive and destructive behaviors in life are sort of least-common-denominator choices; they're really not that hard to make, and pretty much every human being is capable of recognizing and making them.

TO THINK OR NOT TO THINK?

To me, our unique ability to think about our behavior—to differentiate between constructive and destructive and to choose
the constructive over the destructive—implies a duty to do so,
but not everyone agrees. As we saw in Chapter 3, some people's
brains are working plenty well enough to choose the constructive,
yet they go right ahead and choose the destructive anyway. Even
more people simply choose not to think at all and to base their
behavioral choices instead solely on what feels good to them in
the moment. It's easy to see why I call the former choice (in a non-
religious sense) "evil," but I call the latter choice "evil" as well. It's
like saying, "Thanks but no thanks for my humanity; I'll just be
an animal, let my actions be governed by physiology and/or emotion, and thus have no moral obligation or accountability rather
than actually use my intellect to differentiate right from wrong."

For example, if a mole tears up your front lawn by digging tun-
nels through it, there's no moral failing. The animal is incapable
of weighing the impact of that destructive behavior upon you.
But if a human teenager tears up your front lawn by deliberately
driving a car through it ("farms your yard," as they say in my
home state of Kansas), that's wrong, even if the teenager didn't
stop to think about the impact on you. The fact is, any remotely
normal teenager could've, and therefore should've, thought about
that impact and avoided that destructive behavior. Human beings
don't get to escape moral obligation or accountability by simply
turning off their intellect. This is a major reason why, by the
way, I'm not a big fan of recreational intoxication with any substance, legal or illegal—the whole point of which is to dim one's

intellect. If you can't fully enjoy yourself while you're fully conscious, then you have serious issues that you need address with
your intellect fully intact.

So every human being with a minimally functional intellect can
think, and therefore, they can own, but not everyone's equally so
inclined. Why not? What makes some of us more likely to continue
moaning even as our intellects develop beyond early childhood,
while others of us stop moaning and start owning? For starters,
the messages that we get—or don't get—from our parents have
profound effects on how likely we are to stop moaning and start
owning as we grow physiologically from highly dependent infants
into highly independent adults.

WHO'S IN CONTROL?

As I brought up in Chapter 2, most of the major life lessons
about behavior, our mastery of which largely determines how successful we'll be in living and working among other human beings
throughout our lives, are mastered—or not—in early childhood:

- Don't hit. Control yourself even when you're unhappy.
- Don't take what isn't yours. Control yourself even when
  you want things.
- If you make a mess, clean it up. When it *is* your fault,
  be accountable.

When our parents teach us those lessons, they're really teaching
us to think about our behavior, about its impact on others, and
to make value judgments about behavior—that certain behaviors
are better than others. As I also mentioned in Chapter 2, one's

propensity to delay gratification—or not—tends to be internalized in early childhood. When our parents make us wait and work for things that we want, they teach us to think about what we need and want in life, to differentiate between needs and wants, and to develop healthy tolerances for unfulfilled wants.

To this list of lessons and tendencies learned—or not—primarily from our parents in early childhood, add a fundamental personality trait called *locus of control*. First coined by psychologist Julian Rotter in the 1950s, locus of control refers to where one believes the control over one's life lies along a continuum ranging from completely external to completely internal. One who develops a totally external locus of control believes there's nothing one can do to affect how one's life plays out. Life is like floating on the ocean in an oar-less, sail-less raft; one must just hope that fair winds and warm currents carry one to good places. At the other extreme of the continuum, one who develops a totally internal locus of control believes one not only can affect but can actually determine how every aspect of one's life plays out.

Both extremes along the continuum can be dysfunctional. Those at the external extreme wish for things to go their way in life, but their wishes are profoundly less likely to come true when they take no proactive steps toward self-fulfillment; they end up doing a lot of moaning and no owning. For example, instead of furthering his education, an eighteen-year-old who wishes to have a nice car and a nice house and money in the bank someday may get a full-time job waiting tables and use some of his tip money to buy lottery tickets each week, thinking that there's no point in striving for a better life; life's about the luck of the draw. Those at the internal extreme are highly proactive, but they have difficulty accepting that realities of life—like other people's wants, needs, feelings, and behaviors in relationships—truly are not controllable. While they do a lot of owning, they may still find themselves feeling unhappy and moaning. For example, a skilled young surgeon who is accustomed to having procedures go as expected may blame himself the first time he loses a patient, thinking that there must have been something he should've foreseen or something he should've done differently, no matter how poor the patient's prognosis had been.

Locus of Control

External	Moaners	Owners	Internal

The truth is that we're not in complete control of how our lives play out, but if we're proactive, we have a lot of power to affect a lot of our outcomes. Most successful people consciously or subconsciously recognize this, which is why most successful people tend to fall toward the internal end of the locus-of-control continuum. Instead of moaning about others, or about life in general not making them happy, not handing them things they need and want, or blaming them unfairly for their failings, they tend to own their roles in causing or fixing those outcomes. In short, it's good to have a relatively internal locus of control. People who have one tend to do less moaning and more owning and to go further in life by just about every measure (in school, in their relationships, and in their careers).

The distinction is clear in the aftermath of events like the terrorist attacks of September 11, 2001. Virtually all of us want to think that nothing's going to drop from the sky and kill thousands of people, so when it happens, it creates what psychologists call *cognitive dissonance*—that uncomfortable feeling we get when what we're experiencing is inconsistent with what we want to think. An individual American's locus of control is predictive, then, of what that person will do to resolve that dissonance. Someone with an internal locus of control is more likely to try to restore a sense that what happens in life is predictable based on their behavior. They may therefore go to the attack site to try to help with rescue and recovery efforts, they may go to a local blood bank and donate blood, or they may go to their local recruitment center and join the military to help defend the nation from future attacks. Someone with an external locus of control, on the other hand, is more likely to simply resign themselves to the idea that life has just become that unpredictable. Accordingly, they may be more prone to turn to alcohol or drugs to merely escape from the frightening reality of the situation. And, writing in the *Huffington Post* in 2013, self-described "poor person" Linda Tirado illustrated the relationship between locus of control and delay of gratification better than I ever could.[29] Here's a sampling of particularly illustrative parts of her article:

"We have learned not to try too hard to be middle-class . . . Better not to try."

"Junk food is a pleasure that we are allowed to have; why would we give that up?"

"I smoke. It's expensive. It's also the best option . . . I can smoke and I feel a little better, just for a minute."

"I make a lot of poor financial decisions. None of them
   matter, in the long term. I will never not be poor . . ."

"It's not like the sacrifice will result in improved
   circumstances . . .

"It is not worth it to me to live a bleak life devoid of
   small pleasures so that one day I can make a single large
   purchase . . ."

"There's a certain pull to live what bits of life you can
   while there's money in your pocket, because no matter
   how responsible you are you will be broke in three days
   anyway."

"We don't plan long-term because if we do we'll just get
   our hearts broken. It's best not to hope. You just take
   what you can get as you spot it."

While I admire Ms. Tirado's honesty about how an external
locus of control correlates with a tendency not to delay gratification, I worry about the chances of her *children* developing an
internal locus of control. Children are more likely to develop an
internal locus of control when their parents model it and focus on
developing the children's sense of self-efficacy (the sense that one
can do and get things for oneself) than self-esteem. This means
letting their egos—as well as their knees and elbows—get bruised
so that they learn they can recover, letting them fail so that they
learn they can turn around and succeed, letting them solve their
own problems so that they learn they can tolerate frustration and
function independently. The ironic upshot of self-efficacy is that
it promotes self-reliance, which promotes self-regulation, which

promotes self-confidence, which promotes self-improvement (i.e., initiative), of which healthy self-*esteem* ultimately is an outgrowth or a byproduct.

PARENTS VS. FRIENDS

We're less likely to moan and more likely to own when our parents teach us early in life that it's important to think about our behavior, that certain behaviors are better than others, that we have the ability to choose our behaviors, and that the choices we make will greatly affect the outcomes that we experience in life. To teach those lessons, though, parents have to be present and involved in their children's lives; they have to set behavioral boundaries for their children—that is, say no to their children, often, until their children exhibit healthy self-regulation skills; they have to hold their children accountable, and rather than helicoptering in to rescue them, let the children experience negative consequences when they behave destructively; and they have to proactively articulate, explain, and model behavioral standards for their children. In short, they have to be, first and foremost, parents, not friends.

In my work with teenagers over the years, I've continually been surprised by how many of their mothers, especially in affluent families, seemed to treat their teenage girls less as minor daughters and more as adult "gal pals." When I see sixteen-year-old girls dressed like twenty-five-year-olds, driving luxury cars and sports cars like twenty-five-year-olds (twenty-five-year-olds with well-paying jobs!), drinking (with their mothers' knowledge, permission, and often facilitation), and so on, it's really no wonder that the girls feel ready to be sexually active like twenty-five-year-olds.

I wrote in Part I about how some of my colleagues in the behavioral sciences have been unhelpful to Americans in certain ways, and here's yet another: For years now, so-called experts, who often seem inexplicably unconcerned about sexual activity among kids in their early teens, have been citing highly questionable research to suggest that it's pointless to tell kids to delay sexual activity. Well, better research has now confirmed what I've said all along: When adults whom they respect tell them that it's smart, and *why* it's smart, to put off putting out, teens do listen—they may not say so, but they do—and they're more likely to delay sexual activity than are kids whose sexual advice from adults is all about how to do it "safely."[30] Dads, listen up: The research shows that if you're present and involved in your daughters' daily lives, you, in particular, may have the ability to serve as that little voice in their heads when they need an excuse to decline to participate in something for which they're not ready.

THE FOURTH "R": REASONING

Schools play a role, too. Ideally, they reinforce what parents are doing at home, but when parents abdicate the responsibilities outlined above, schools can at least serve as partial substitutes. Kids are more likely to own when schools teach critical thinking, when they teach students that it's not enough to just understand a dilemma (e.g., to understand each of two mutually exclusive behavioral options); it's important to then be able to solve the dilemma (to identify the more productive option). This outcome, of course, requires acknowledgment within the school that certain behaviors are better than others. Over my years of working with young people, I've observed this approach less often in public schools, where many teachers are afraid to make value judgments, and more often in parochial schools.

I recall counseling a public high school student years ago on the Monday after his school's spring break. Over the break, another student from his school had died in a multistory fall while drunkenly attempting to climb from one hotel balcony to another. When classes resumed at the school that Monday, word of the death quickly spread throughout the student body, and the students understandably wanted to talk about it with one another and with their teachers. I sat in stunned, appalled disbelief when the student told me that one of his teachers had admonished him for bringing up the fact that alcohol had been involved in the death, telling him, "Don't speak ill of the dead." Had that teacher not been so ridiculously afraid to acknowledge that sobriety is better, or at least safer, than intoxication, particularly for minors, she might've actually been able to extract a future lifesaving lesson from a tragedy. Instead, she made the kid sitting across from me feel bad about himself, simply because he had identified profoundly destructive behavior for what it was.

Kids are also less likely to moan and more likely to own when schools teach the historical and economic virtues of owning, for example, how owners, not moaners, built America and how capitalism promotes and rewards owning, not moaning. In addition, kids are less likely to moan and more likely to own when schools give them credit where credit is *earned*, and where it's not earned, let them experience the consequences—low scores, disappointment, extra work, and so on—whether in the class-room, on the athletic field, or on the performance stage. At the same time, kids are less likely to moan and more likely to own when schools—often the first communities to which kids feel they belong, apart from their families—teach kids the importance of considering the impact of their actions, for better or worse, on the other community members.

I recall another high school student from years ago, this one from a parochial school, who told me about a classmate who had committed violation after violation of the school's code of student conduct—fighting, vandalism, profanity directed toward staff—yet had been allowed to remain enrolled in the school. The disillusioned student sitting in my office asked me why, under the circumstances, he should worry about keeping his own behavior in line with the code of conduct, and I had to tell him I didn't have a good answer, but I'd get him one. The next day, I called the school's principal, explained my student's understandable disillu-sionment, and asked what I should tell the student. The response was, "Who would Jesus expel?"

In stunned disbelief again, I said back to the principal, "Well, first of all, as I understand Christianity, I don't think Jesus ever wanted to be a principal, or a president, or any similar public administrator enforcing the rules of any earthly community, but that doesn't necessarily mean Jesus didn't think such roles and rules were necessary. So, while I believe that Jesus probably wouldn't have wanted to expel anybody and that Jesus certainly would've been concerned about a clearly troubled student, I also believe Jesus would've been concerned about the many students whose educations were being compromised by the one problem student, having their classes repeatedly disrupted and their respect for the school's behavioral standards undermined." The problem student was gone after that semester—better late than never.

THE CHOICE IS OURS

It helps us to own when our parents and educators encourage us to think, particularly about our behavior and its impact upon others, and when they hold us accountable if we fail to think. But even if we don't have those advantages growing up, as long as we reach adulthood with minimally functional intellects, we can *choose* whether to moan or to own. We can choose to consciously be part of things larger than ourselves. Paraphrasing President John F. Kennedy, we can choose to ask not what others can do for us but what we can do for others. And we can choose, in spite of cultural deterrents, to make value judgments about behavior (our own and others') based on how it impacts those larger things. When we're not afraid to do so, we (and others) are more likely to own.

JUDGMENT CALLS

Whenever someone criticizes me for being "judgmental" on the air, I always ask, "So, if your daughter's boyfriend or husband cheats on her, are you seriously going to tell her that infidelity's just a 'different choice' that's no worse and no better than fidelity?" And unless they're clinically insane, everyone replies, "No, of course I'm going to tell her she should dump the jerk!" Okay, good, then we're on the same page. Judgments about behavior aren't just acceptable, they're absolutely necessary for humans to live constructively among one another in relationships, families, schools, businesses, communities, and nations.

America's Founding Fathers understood this well (and so, I believe, did Jesus). They knew that we'd never have enough cops or soldiers on our streets to ensure that most people most of the time did most things right (and that if we ever did have that kind of big-brother government, we'd no longer be free). Instead, they realized that in a free society, social mores, good people making judgments about behavior, and imposing commensurate social (rather than physical or legal) consequences would do far more than government could ever do to encourage constructive behavior and discourage destructive behavior.

We can also choose to surround ourselves with people who tend to own rather than moan, which makes us, and them, more likely to own in the future. A longitudinal lifestyle study spanning eight decades called the Longevity Project summed it up this way: "The groups you associate with often determine the type of person you become."[31] In other words, choose to associate more with moaners, and you're more likely to moan; choose to associate more with owners, and you're more likely to own. This is true both in one's immediate personal and professional life and in our broader local, regional, and national communities.

A TALE OF TWO FLOODS

For instance, in 2008 I appeared on a national evening newscast from St. Louis, Missouri, after having a chance to visit some flood-ravaged areas along the Mississippi River. As I was looking at partially submerged buildings and light poles, and flooded streets and farms, I was reminded of all the video I'd seen leading up to, during, and in the aftermath of this flood, and I couldn't help comparing it to my memories of video coming out of New Orleans before, during, and after Hurricane Katrina. In both places (the Midwest and New Orleans), like most places inhabited by human beings, the vast majority of the inhabitants were thankfully able-bodied, able-minded, good, and decent people. In both places, the populations knew for days that devastating floods were likely to come. But there also were some critical differences between the two places.

In one place, many of the inhabitants seemed to do relatively little to prepare for the rising waters, while in the other place it seemed like the entire community pretty much banded together, stacked sandbags upon sandbags for days upon days, and where it became apparent that those efforts were futile, helped one another pack up their essentials and whatever else could be safely salvaged. In one place, some inhabitants who weren't able-bodied were left to die, unable to flee the rising waters, while in the other place, as far as I know, the able-bodied inhabitants made sure that fellow inhabitants in need of evacuation assistance got it. In one place, many people ended up on rooftops, waiting for others in helicopters or rescue boats to come and save them from the rising waters after the flood, while in the other place, I recall seeing just a couple such rescues because the vast majority of the inhabitants had gotten themselves to higher ground before the floodwaters arrived.

In one place, many people died, while in the other place, I don't know of anyone who did (some may have, I just don't know about it). In one place, some of the remaining inhabitants stole the possessions of those who had fled to higher ground, not just essentials for survival like food items, but luxury items like big-screen TVs; in the other place, I don't know of anyone who did (again, some may have, but if they did, I don't know about it). In one place, some of the remaining inhabitants were raped and even killed by other remaining inhabitants, while in the other place, I don't know of anyone who was (and I'm confident that I would've heard about that). In one place, people were angry that their fellow Americans weren't doing enough for them while they were displaced, while in the other place, I didn't hear a single person be anything other than appreciative of any help that had been received. In one place, many of the inhabitants had remained displaced for years, still angry, still bitter, still demanding things of others, while in the other place, all I saw was an eagerness to get back into the flooded areas, roll up their sleeves, rebuild, and get on with life as soon as possible.

So what was it about the populations of these two places that made such a profound relative difference in how they dealt with similar (although not identical) circumstances? First, let me say what wasn't: It wasn't demographics. Differences in racial, educational, religious, and population-density statistics didn't explain it. What explained it, I believe, was the difference between rural and urban environments in the sense of self vis-a-vis community. Many people in the flooded areas of the Midwest exhibited, on average (with notable exceptions), a fairly internal locus of control, while people in New Orleans exhibited, on average (again with notable exceptions), a fairly external locus of control.[32]

Midwesterners, therefore, seemed to have a strong dispositional tendency not to see themselves as victims of circumstance (i.e., to reject the notion of having little or no control) and thus to own that which they could control (even when things beyond their control were happening), which resulted largely in their not becoming victims of much other than water damage to property (which can cause profound economic suffering as well as some emotional suffering, from the loss of sentimental possessions, for example, but it's not the same as losing loved ones). Many people in New Orleans, on the other hand, seemed to be less averse to assuming the victim role and thus to wait for others to own and assert control over their circumstances, which resulted not only in their being victims of profound physical, economic, and emotional suffering due to the floodwaters, but also of the crimes perpetrated by the sociopaths who took advantage of the situation.

It seems to me that farming communities tend to socialize kids to be self-reliant and resilient and to believe that what they reap in life (figuratively and literally) will be no more and no less than what they sow. At the same time, it seems to me that some of our urban communities, particularly where there's poverty combined with corruption, as there historically has been in New Orleans (bankrupt Detroit is another prime example), socialize kids to be dependent on others, particularly government (i.e., politicians), and to believe that what they get out of life will essentially be what they can get from someone else. I'm oversimplifying this, but it's in the interest of getting to the bottom line: I've never seen any able-bodied, able-minded person be helped by encouragement to be dependent on others for the basic necessities of life, to see himself or herself as a victim, or to be comfortable in the victim role. Choosing to surround ourselves with others—family members, friends, colleagues, church members, and fellow citizens—who tend to own instead of moan makes us more likely to do the same (and vice versa).

PEER PRESSURE

Unfortunately, not all of us have parents who encourage us to think of ourselves as part of things larger, to think about our behavior and its impacts upon others, and who help us to develop self-efficacy, self-reliance, self-confidence, and initiative—in other words, to own. As we've seen time and time again in this book, many parents, consciously or subconsciously, encourage their children to moan. Some actively nurture entitlement by aggrandizing their children unconditionally, overindulging their children, or absolving their children of accountability, while others passively model entitlement by neglecting their children.

And not all of us have educators and other role models during our formative years who teach us to own rather than to moan. As we've also seen earlier in this book, many of today's American schools, youth sports teams, and others fail to teach the competitive and cooperative virtues of owning over moaning—that moaning doesn't make productive individual citizens or individual players, nor does moaning make productive communities or teams; owning does. Instead, they too often prioritize self-esteem over self-efficacy, give credit where credit isn't due, and refuse to hold students accountable for behavior that's destructive to those students' personal and educational development or to others.

And even though, by the time we're adults, we're virtually all nevertheless capable of choosing to think of ourselves in broader social context, to think about the effects of our behavior, and to own instead of moan, not all of us are so inclined. With ample encouragement from popular culture, too many Americans choose to view their lives as if they're the stars of their own personal biopics in which everyone else on Earth is, at best, a supporting character, if not just an extra. When life doesn't go their way, and others don't give them what they want, they choose to moan rather than own, to take rather than give, to externalize blame rather than admit fault, and they tend to surround themselves, for the most part, with like-minded people. Can even these people stop moaning and start owning? Yes!

How can that happen? First, let me tell you how it probably won't happen. Much as I'd like to report otherwise, it's highly unlikely that even the best therapist—let alone a spouse, friend, or colleague—is going to talk a moaning adult into owning. Nobody comes into a therapist's office and says, "I'm [insert your favorite term for a moaner: narcissistic, entitled, antisocial, . . .], and I want help to be a better person." Adult moaners generally have little or no intrinsic motivation to change, and even their responses to extrinsic motivation—for example, a court order to seek therapy—tend to be largely self-serving and superficial. They may go through the motions of showing up and telling the therapist what they think the therapist wants to hear, but their motivation and manipulation tend to be about getting the process over with, not about getting their character overhauled.

As we've seen earlier in this book, the internalization of empathy for others and a sense of duty to others tends to happen, if at all, in childhood. If someone makes it to adulthood, or even late adolescence, without having internalized those things, even though they retain the capacity to do so, the likelihood of them actually doing so, sadly, isn't high. Those rare individuals who do acquire genuine motivation to get into therapy and make sustained efforts to change fundamental aspects of their character seem to always have undergone devastating life experiences stemming from narcissism, entitlement, and sociopathy, such as incarceration, estrangement of a spouse or children, ruination of a career, and so on, and even then, it generally takes months if not years to make meaningful progress.

This is where a broader community can play an important role in encouraging people to stop moaning and start owning through public policy. If individuals aren't experiencing motivating social consequences for their moaning behavior from those with whom they choose to surround themselves (because they tend to surround themselves with other moaners), society at large can step in and supply such consequences. The motivation will be extrinsic—that is, it probably won't cause anyone to internalize principled thoughts that weren't instilled in them as children and that they haven't chosen to embrace as adults—but it can motivate people to at least act less like moaners and more like owners. It's just behaviorism. Moaners behave in self-interested ways, so if society makes it be in their self-interest to stop moaning and start owning, they're more likely to do so.

RUSSELL'S SILVER RULE

Remember my Silver Rule (the golden one's taken): "You don't get people to do more of the right thing by making it easier for them to do the wrong thing." As a society, if we want less moaning, we can make moaning harder, so that owning, at least to a minimally functional degree, becomes the behavioral path of least resistance. For instance, in virtually every society that offers its citizens unemployment benefits, dramatically elevated percentages of benefit recipients tend to find jobs right around the time when the benefits run out.[33] So, there's apparently a huge motivational factor in play, whereby many recipients appear to wait until their benefits are close to running out before they really become serious about looking for work or bring their expectations about the kinds of work they'd prefer into line with the kind of work that's actually available to them. Thus, had we increased the duration of benefits beyond two years (recall back in Chapter 2, a recipient threatened the life of the Speaker of the House demanding that extension), we would likely have delayed the point at which the motivation factor kicked in for many recipients—with notable exceptions, of course—and actually prolonged their unemployment.

Behavioral economics dictates that independent human beings are most productive when they're left to do as much for themselves as possible and left to keep as much of what they produce as possible. As soon as they start having things done for them that they could do for themselves or having more taken from them than absolutely necessary (e.g., necessary to defend and preserve the nation), they become less productive than they could be. These simple axioms have profound public policy implications in the areas of taxation and spending (i.e., wealth redistribution) for any nation, state, or community that wants its citizens to stop moaning and start owning and to be as productive and self-reliant as possible. Behaviorism isn't just key to understanding how to make effective public policy when it comes to economics; it's also key to understanding how to effectively deter crime.

I've assessed numerous criminals over the years, and I've been involved in the television coverage of most major national crime stories for the better part of a decade, so take it from me: if someone has made it out of childhood without internalizing, for example, that it's wrong to steal, you're probably never going to talk the person into embracing that value (into actually feeling bad about taking and enjoying other people's property). If you're like me, that's probably hard for you to imagine. I have a PhD in psychology, and I still don't really understand it. If I walked out of a store with something I hadn't paid for, I'd feel so guilty and ashamed and scared of being thought a thief that I couldn't possibly keep and enjoy whatever I had taken. But for narcissistic, entitled sociopaths, it's easy; they don't think about the people who worked for the stolen item and about how the theft affects them, and while we're not likely to talk them into caring about such things, we *can* get them to stop stealing.

How do we do that? Not by giving them second, third, or fourth chances to steal, but by imposing swift and relatively severe negative consequences for the first theft and by credibly threatening escalating consequences for a second theft so that it's in their own selfish best interests not to steal again. Just as toddlers in Kohlberg's preconventional stage of character development (discussed in Chapter 2) need swift behavioral feedback, including consequences aversive enough to convey the message that a behavior is unacceptable and to promote sustained positive behavior change, adults who essentially never make it out of that stage sadly continue to need the same, but at an adult level (more on this in Chapter 6). And when they get such feedback and consequences, it's actually better for them as well as for society in the long run.

For example, in the spring of 2014, not far from where I live, employees at a twenty-four-hour grocery store heard strange noises emanating from above the tiles of the store's drop ceiling. Something appeared to be moving around up there. The employees called 911, and the local police came and searched the premises. After an hour of searching, they found a thirty-seven-year-old man hiding in the ceiling—but that's not all he had done. He had figured out how to enter the ceiling in a publicly accessible part of the store (a restroom), then crawl over to the part of the ceiling above the store's pharmacy, then drop down into the pharmacy after pharmacy hours and steal prescription drugs. He eventually pled guilty to breaking into the pharmacy and to the theft of the drugs, and what did he get? Probation. Thirty-six months on probation, plus an order to pay the grocery store $7,000 for its damage and losses.

In explaining her rationale for such a lenient sentence, the judge referred to a drug and alcohol assessment submitted by the defense and said to the defendant, "It is apparent this crime occurred because of your addiction."[34] Let me get this straight— burglary's not as bad if the burglar's addicted to whatever he stole? No, Judge, this crime did not happen because of the defendant's "addiction." Nobody, no matter how badly they want something to make them feel good, is forced to commit a crime to get it. Otherwise, we'd have to let people who say they're addicted to golf get by with trespassing on private golf courses. Or, far more serious, we'd have to let people who say they're addicted to sex get by with rape. Many people want many pleasurable things badly, yet they restrain themselves from committing crimes to get those things. A civil society must expect such behavior from everyone.

This crime happened because of narcissistic entitlement. The defendant wanted something that belonged to someone else, the defendant either couldn't or didn't want to go to the trouble to get it honestly, and the defendant felt entitled to violate the private property rights of the owner and the laws of our state by taking it. It's that simple. (Moreover, if the defendant was addicted to prescription drugs, unless he got addicted while using those drugs in strict compliance with valid prescriptions, he likely committed prior crimes such as possessing and using a controlled substance without a prescription.)

In accepting the addiction excuse and meting out so little punishment, the judge essentially told this defendant that my community's fine with what he did. Well, I'm not fine with it. The judge seems to have been more concerned about the defendant than about the rest of us in the community whom the defendant might harm next time he decides to break into someone's private property and steal something. And who seriously thinks that this defendant, even given the entire rest of his life, is ever going to pay the $7,000 to the grocery store? Not I. But even if he does pay it back, where's the effective disincentive to steal when all one has to do, if caught, is pay the property owner back? I would've sentenced the defendant to prison for at least thirty-six months and then to probation lasting at least until he paid back the $7,000, with interest. That sentence would've made it far less likely that my local police would be having to apprehend this same defendant again in the near future. Even if the loss of years of his life and the prospect of an even harsher sentence next time didn't deter him, at least he wouldn't have been loose in my community to commit any more crimes for a significant period of time. (And if the prison were run like I would run it, such that no illicit drugs were accessible to the inmates, a significant prison sentence also could've solved the defendant's substance abuse problem.)

TOUGH LOVE

It has been chronically frustrating to see how the vast majority of crimes that I've analyzed on TV could have been prevented had we, as a society, intervened sooner, more severely, and longer in the perpetrators' lives when we had prior chances to do so. Even for mentally ill offenders whose ability to think clearly about their behavior may be compromised, consequences are key. Unless they're threatening to do imminent harm to themselves or others, our mental health system is largely powerless to keep them off the streets. That's why, when they commit crimes, it's really not compassionate—certainly not to the innocent people whom they might harm, and generally not to the offenders themselves—for the criminal justice system to give them passes. Criminal charges open the door for society to intervene broadly in their lives, via judges with the power to order mental status evaluations and then either confine them or release them conditionally (e.g., upon agreement to have them participate in any recommended treatment, take medications as prescribed, refrain from substance abuse, and submit to location monitoring, drug testing, court supervision, etc.), and subject them to immediate re-arrest should they violate the conditions. Then, once their mental status has been ascertained, if there's strong evidence of profound impairment, prosecution can always be diverted or deferred, again conditionally (e.g., upon agreement to have the defendant complete a course of inpatient hospitalization with longitudinal outpatient follow-up and supervision postrelease) and subject to conviction and sentencing should they violate the conditions.

The bottom line is that virtually all of us can own. We own when we think, and we think when we're motivated to do so. It's best when our motivation to own is intrinsic—rooted in good parenting and good schooling and reinforced by mature choices to view ourselves as parts of things larger, to care about how our behavior affects those things larger, and to surround ourselves with others who do likewise. But even when people resist thinking in those terms (and in the statistically rare cases in which adults are prevented from doing so consistently because of profound neurological impairments), society can often provide extrinsic motivation to own, at least to a minimally functional degree.

The transformative power of the choice to own our failures and challenges in this life is enormous. When we make it individually, it's the choice to be the best people we can be, and when we make it collectively, it's the choice to be the best society we can be.

PART III:

START
OWNING!

CHAPTER 6

The Power of Personal Responsibility

The best years of your life are the ones
in which you decide your problems are your own.
You do not blame them on your mother, the ecology,
or the president. You realize that you
control your own destiny.

—Albert Ellis

THE ENTITLEMENT ANTIDOTE

Part II of this book was about how moaning is rooted in entitlement while owning is rooted in personal responsibility (the antithesis of entitlement), the conditions under

which we moan, and the conditions under which we stop moaning
and start owning. Part III is about what happens after we stop
moaning and start owning—when we replace entitlement with
personal responsibility. We get happier, we experience more of
our needs and wants as being fulfilled, and we retake control of
our destinies.

Personal responsibility has a ripple effect that makes us, and
our country, better in the following ways:

- Personally responsible individuals make better relationship
  partners.
- Personally responsible parents raise better children.
- Personally responsible colleagues build better
  organizations.
- Personally responsible citizens build better communities
  and a better country.

Personal responsibility has two component parts. First, it has
a retrospective component, *accountability* for destructive behavior in the past, which empowers us to benefit ourselves and each
other through its second, prospective, component: the *obligation*
to behave constructively in the future.

THE POWER OF ACCOUNTABILITY

I've worked with many people who've been addicted to various substances, most of whom have recounted chronic cycles
of abuse punctuated by temporary periods of abstinence. In
recounting those cycles, virtually all of them understandably have
used words like "disease" and "relapse." As I said earlier, these

are responsibility-absolving words that medicalize the problem and equate it with cellular diseases like cancer, which sometimes spontaneously reoccur after sustained periods of remission. Such medical terminology is part of the predominant addiction-treatment lexicon and philosophy in America today. Unfortunately, that particular philosophy hasn't been very successful in actually helping people remain abstinent. If you average the results of numerous treatment programs employing this disease philosophy, you'll find that about 80 percent of participants abstain only briefly and then resume substance abuse.[35] Therefore, I believe, at least with a high percentage of addicts, we have to try something new—more accurately, something old: personal responsibility.

FROM ACCOUNTABILITY TO OBLIGATION

Even if one insists upon conceptualizing the mental component of addiction—the desire for the destructive substance—as a disease over which the person has no control, when it comes to the behavioral component (the actual consumption of the substance), there's always a choice. And just as addiction itself has mental and behavioral components, addiction treatment has mental and behavioral components—the mental component being recognition that there's a choice involved, and the behavioral component being abstinence.

When treatment programs encourage addicts to conceptualize their addictions as diseases, and themselves as victims thereof, it's actually quite disempowering.[36] As I discussed earlier in the book, if addiction were a disease—something that strikes a person without warning, like a lightning bolt out of a clear blue sky—then how can a person feel any real sense of self-efficacy to solve the problem, let alone self-confidence in the ability to prevent recurrences of it? It would be like getting in your car and discovering that it drives itself and you are just the passenger, helplessly letting it take you where it wants to go. No one forces a person to take a drink and keep on drinking, or light up a cigarette and keep on smoking. But it's not easy for someone to own up to his or her role in initiating and perpetuating a pattern of destructive behavior.

With ownership, however, comes empowerment. Anyone who really wants to quit smoking, drinking, shooting heroin, overeating, and so on has the power to quit doing those things; many millions have done it. That's the power of personal responsibility and what I think ought to be the starting presumption of any addiction treatment. If someone's choices caused his or her problem, then making different choices can solve the problem. As I said in Chapter 5, I believe that an *ability* to make different choices translates into a *duty* to make different choices. Addicts and other subscribers to the disease philosophy of addiction love to say it's not a moral issue. Yes, it is.

Most of us know others who've successfully quit all kinds of addictive behaviors. Did they tend to quit—and stay quit—when counselors in rehab programs talked them into it? No. Those counselors too often are former substance abusers themselves, and in my opinion, they're the last people who ought to be counseling addicts. Addicts don't need to hear from people who can relate to their destructive desires; they need to hear precisely from people who *can't* relate to those desires, people who, rather than making the same destructive choices, have consistently made diametrically different, healthier choices. Addicts tend to quit when something changes that finally prompts them to choose between short-term and long-term gratification, and they choose long-term. A child says, "I'm afraid you're going to die if you don't quit." An employer says, "I'm not going to pay for your health insurance if you don't quit." A spouse says, "I'm leaving you if you don't quit." Something happens that shifts the addicts' temporal frame of reference from short-term to long-term and causes them to consider the risk implications of their behavior in the aggregate—say, the next fifteen years—rather than just the immediate, the next fifteen minutes. With this change in perspective, the previously rational becomes irrational, and the irresistible becomes sustainably resistible. In short, they quit when they finally choose to value something or someone else over their addictions.

Unfortunately, there aren't great comparison data for the effectiveness of this alternative approach to addiction. Why? Because when addicts finally do quit for good, not just temporarily, they often do so without professional assistance—not in the context of any treatment program. So, it's tough to know how many millions of Americans have successfully beaten addictions because they essentially chose to stop moaning and start owning, but I'd bet they amount to many times the number of Americans who've successfully beaten addictions because they've completed rehab programs based on the disease philosophy.

I'm not recommending against professional assistance when someone's trying to beat an addiction. Particularly when physiological withdrawal symptoms are possible, they may still need professional assistance with the psychophysiological repercussions of quitting. I'm simply saying that once an addict owns his or her addictive behavior and chooses to think about its long-term impact on what and whom they truly value, more than the short-term gratification that they *feel* from the addiction, they tend not to need much convincing to quit. Likewise, they tend not to want to sit around and moan about their addictions much longer; they'd rather not waste more of their precious time.

Even if you think that addiction is a disease and that an addict's personal responsibility for his or her condition is the same as that of a leukemia patient, when it comes to stopping the addictive behavior, there's simply nothing to be gained from focusing on anything that you think is beyond their control. If we really want to succeed in helping addicts quit, then we need to focus our efforts on what is within their control. Think about a different kind of problem, like lightning striking someone's house and starting a fire that burns it down. We can probably agree that the homeowner didn't have any control over the lightning, but if the homeowner wants to rebuild the house and avoid a recurrence of that disaster (yes, lightning does strike twice in the same place), then it's pointless to focus on the uncontrollability of the lightning. Focusing on that would only reinforce an external locus of control, promote a sense of helplessness, and deter the homeowner from taking productive action. Instead, the focus needs to be on what the homeowner *can* control. For example, he can rebuild with more flame-retardant materials, he can install a sprinkler system in the rebuilt house, and he can install a lightning rod system on the rebuilt house. Focusing on that will reinforce an internal locus of control, promote a sense of self-efficacy, and encourage productive action. The same goes for addicts.

While it may be difficult and unpleasant, *accountability*—taking personal responsibility for what we've done or not done in the past—empowers us to do something different and better in the future. This is where *obligation*—taking personal responsibility to behave productively in the future—kicks in. Just as one who's accountable for addictive behavior in the past is then both empowered and obligated to remain abstinent in the future, one who's accountable for what they have not had in the past is then both empowered and obligated to become more content with what they have in the future (which may mean producing more, prioritizing better, or a combination of the two).

PRESCRIPTION FOR PERSONAL PROSPERITY

Perhaps the most poignant illustration of the power of personal responsibility that I can offer you in this book is my eight-point Prescription for Personal Prosperity, made up of four don'ts and four dos. If the lawyers would've let me, I would've given a money-back guarantee, right here in this book, that an able-bodied, able-minded young person who adheres to just the first four points of this prescription—the don'ts—will always be able to provide themselves and their immediate family with life's basic necessities here in America:

1. **Don't commit any crimes.** I don't just mean no murders, rapes, or armed robberies; I mean *no* crimes whatsoever. Even driving drunk one time risks irreversible damage to yourself and others. Those with criminal records are

dramatically more likely to experience unemployment and poverty than those without criminal records. Even when they haven't lost substantial time out of their productive lives to incarceration, job applicants with criminal records tend to be among employers' least preferred applicants, and rightly so. Employers have limited information with which to make high-stakes predictions about how job applicants, if hired, will treat the employers' customers, other employees, and property. Thus, as an expert in human behavior and the law, I'll testify on behalf of virtually any employer, anytime, that information about an applicant's past disregard for the law is cause for reasonable concern about future disregard for the law, perhaps of the same or even a more serious type as in the past. Accordingly, job applicants with criminal records tend to have much harder times finding jobs, and when they do, they tend to land significantly lower-paying jobs than competitors without criminal records. In addition, many educational institutions and occupational licensing authorities deny admission or licensure to applicants with criminal records. So, just obey the law. It's not hard; in fact, you should easily be able to go through your entire lifetime without committing a single offense that interferes with any educational and occupational opportunities.

2. **Don't get addicted to anything.** I don't just mean no heroin, methamphetamine, or cocaine; I mean *no* addictions whatsoever. Even cigarettes carry high physical and financial costs over time. Addicts are dramatically

more likely than nonaddicts to experience unemployment and poverty. Intoxicants are toxic (hence the term "intoxicant"). Sometimes instantly, and certainly over time, they damage the brain, interfering with cognition, processing speed, mood, motivation, and even basic life-support functions like breathing and heartbeat. They cause peripheral tissue damage throughout the body, which in turn causes all kinds of physical, interpersonal, and professional dysfunction, putting others and oneself at risk of physical and emotional harm, up to and including death. And whether you think recreational drug use is a choice (as I do) or a disease, if you're among those whose brains are genetically wired to experience such pleasure from something that you'd squander everything you ever worked for, die young, and leave behind everyone you ever cared about, then it's smartest to never find out, because you can't get addicted to something that you never try. (While family history of addiction is a clear risk factor, the absence of any such history should give you zero confidence that you lack addiction potential.) Use of intoxicants tends to follow a pattern of escalation. Not only is the "gateway" phenomenon real, but in my clinical experience, I don't think I've ever assessed a crack, meth, or heroin addict who didn't start out with alcohol, then marijuana, generally followed by hallucinogenic mushrooms, ecstasy, acid. . . . Notice also how most of the substances I've just mentioned (all of them in certain quantities and cases, e.g., when driving a car) are *illegal*, and recall (1) above!

3. **Don't drop out of school.** Dropouts are more likely than those who finish high school, and dramatically more likely than those who finish college, to experience unemployment and poverty. The unemployment rate for high school dropouts tends to be approximately 1.5 times that of high school graduates and three times that of college graduates. In addition, as of the last U.S. Census, the average employed dropout earns just over $20,000 per year, which is more than $10,000 below the average employed high school graduate and over $36,000 less than the average employed college graduate. Not surprisingly, then, approximately one-third of dropouts live below the poverty line. Moreover, in the first decade of the twenty-first century, jobs requiring college degrees were being created at a rate approximately three times that of jobs requiring only a high school diploma, meaning that the statistics I've just listed are likely to do nothing but worsen for dropouts in the future. Furthermore, dropouts are significantly more likely than high school graduates to end up as unmarried parents of children, whom they then have difficulty supporting, which leads me to my last don't. . . .

4. **Don't make a baby out of wedlock.** Unwed parentage is arguably the single strongest predictor of poverty in America today. And no, parental cohabitation doesn't equate to marriage. Even if unmarried parents are cohabitating at the time of a child's birth, they're approximately six times more likely than married parents to split up and be single parents by their new child's fifth birthday. This is why I'm not a big fan of living together before marriage;

it can diminish the power of a marriage to sustain two
people's commitment to one another through adversity by
turning the marriage into more of an afterthought than
a solemn decision to blend two people's destinies for life.
Unmarried parents are three to four times more likely
than married parents to experience poverty, and it mustn't
be omitted here that this isn't just about you. It's also
about your child. If you're an unmarried parent, not only
are *you* dramatically more likely to experience poverty,
your *child* is also dramatically more likely to experience
poverty—and to underachieve academically, commit
crimes, abuse substances, drop out of school, and become
a single parent. There are parents of minor children who
are unmarried through no fault of their own (for example,
they have been widowed) and are raising exceptional kids,
but I'm confident that even they would tell you it's not
easy and you never want to make a baby who's going to
be in that situation by default from day one.

So, assuming you're able-bodied and able-minded, if all
you wanted to do was to stay out of poverty in America,
and you took only the four steps that I've just outlined,
then achievement of your goal would be almost a certainty. Your statistical probability of ever living below
the poverty line, at least for any sustained period of time
(excepting periods of time spent in school, between jobs,
etc.), would be infinitesimally low. Try to find an able-bodied, able-minded poor adult in America who hasn't failed
to take at least one of those four steps. While I'm sure you
can find one, I predict you'll also find that they're few and

far between. But if you want to do more than to just stay
out of poverty—if you want to truly prosper in America—
then here are four more steps that I recommend you take:

5. **Do delay gratification.** Differentiate between needs and
wants, think long-term, and tolerate unfulfilled wants
until you can fulfill them in appropriate ways that are
within your means. There's nothing wrong with having
wants. Unfulfilled wants motivate a lot of productive
behavior (imagine an economy in which the only goods
and services produced were necessities of life—probably
not an economy in which you'd prefer to participate over
America's). But you should be able to tolerate unfulfilled
wants and even enjoy the time spent fulfilling them. You
can still do impulsive things—smell the roses or live in the
moment—but in general, on balance, most of the time,
a long-term outlook will benefit you more than a short-
term outlook. John Quincy Adams said, "Patience and
perseverance have a magical effect before which difficulties
disappear and obstacles vanish." Thinking long-term and
delaying gratification will help you to avoid succumbing
to the instant, fleeting gratification that comes—at great
long-term cost, as discussed in (2) above—from addictions. Thinking long-term and delaying gratification also
will help you to avoid the allure of short-term gains that
you might obtain through unethical, if not criminal,
behavior. In addition, thinking long-term and delaying gratification will help you to live within your means
and avoid the pitfall of using easy credit to obtain things
and experiences that have little if any lasting value. To a

striking degree, the ability to delay gratification separates the financially successful from the financially unsuccessful. According to a comparison/contrast study of wealthy versus poor Americans:[37]

- Eighty percent of the wealthy are focused on at least one goal vs. 12 percent of the poor.
- Sixty-three percent of the wealthy spend less than one hour per day on recreational Internet use versus 26 percent of the poor.
- Sixty-seven percent of the wealthy watch one hour or less of television per day versus 23 percent of the poor.

An additionally interesting and, I think, related finding from that same study is that 21 percent of the wealthy are overweight by thirty pounds or more versus 66 percent of the poor (and please, nobody tell me that only the wealthy can get their hands on healthy food).

Other findings of further interest, and also related, include:

- Eighty-three percent of the wealthy attended back-to-school night for their kids versus 13 percent of the poor.
- Twenty-nine percent of the wealthy had one or more children who made the honor roll versus 4 percent of the poor.

6. **Do take personal responsibility for fulfilling your needs and wants in life.** This includes, by the way, the needs and wants of any dependents you choose to create. Throughout this book, we've seen many examples of Americans who, for various reasons ranging from how they were

raised to how they've chosen to view themselves and others, have come to expect others to fulfill not only their
needs but also their wants in life, even when those individuals are perfectly capable of fulfilling at least their needs
and probably also many of their wants. As we've also
seen, their sense of entitlement not only manifests itself in
unjustified resentment and jealousy of others, but it also
prevents those individuals from developing the skills necessary to produce more for themselves and others. Here
again, according to that same comparison/contrast study
of wealthy vs. poor Americans, "Seventy-nine percent of
the wealthy believe they are responsible for their financial condition versus 18 percent of the poor." If you're
an able-bodied, able-minded adult who's not earning as
much as you need or want to earn, then you need to start
doing something that's of greater economic value to others. The laws of supply and demand generally apply to the
labor market just as they apply to markets for products.
If you're earning far less money than many other people
around you, it doesn't mean you're not working hard—
you may be working very hard—but what it probably does
mean is that many people can and will do what you're
doing or there isn't much need or desire for what you're
doing. You need to educate, equip, and position yourself
(yes, you may have to relocate) to do something that fewer
people can or will do or for which there's greater need or
desire. And that's your responsibility, nobody else's—not
your employer's, not your government's—yours. You
can ask for help in life, but when you do, make sure it's

not out of laziness and that you recognize your helper's generosity and either pay it back or "pay it forward" (help someone else similarly) as soon as you're able.

7. **Do be accountable.** Accountability means two things: first, owning and repairing any damage caused by your acts or omissions (rather than externalizing responsibility for that damage as we've seen so many Americans doing throughout this book), and second, keeping your commitments. When I lecture about the psychology of business, I like to point out that fifty years ago, in order to stand above your competitors in just about any business in America, you had to deliver a result that somehow exceeded your customers', clients', or employers' expectations—that went above and beyond in some way. Since then, sadly, so many Americans (some of whom we've seen in this book) have failed to even keep their promises, and American culture has become so reluctant to judge their failures harshly (enabling the lazy and incompetent to remain in business), that today, *you can stand out if you simply, consistently, do what you say you're going to do.* Personally, I think we're a better country when you have to go above and beyond to stand out, when keeping one's promises is the norm, and failure to do so is unsustainable. I recommend that you still strive to go above and beyond as often as possible. But if you want to prosper, personally as well as professionally, then at a minimum you should always do what you say you're going to do and take full personal responsibility for fixing any past or future, intentional or unintentional, failure to do so.

8. **Do make a uniquely positive contribution to something larger than yourself.** In short, if you want to be valued *by* others in life, financially and personally, then be of value *to* others. First you must see yourself as part of something larger—a marriage, a family, a business, a church, a community. This means you recognize that everyone else in the world isn't just a supporting character or extra in a story that's all about you. It means recognizing that others have desires and rights to fulfill needs and wants in life, too, and that whatever time, attention, and love they choose instead to "spend" on you are among the greatest gifts you'll ever receive. That's why I say that our attachments to things in life should be extremely loose compared to our attachments to people. It also means recognizing that you have obligations to those people. First, you have an obligation *not* to behave in ways that are destructive. You can compete with others honestly; that tends to make everyone elevate their games. But you shouldn't break promises, take what doesn't belong to you, ask for help you don't need, exercise your freedoms in ways that impinge upon others' abilities to exercise theirs, or take pleasure in the suffering of others. Second, you have an obligation to behave in ways that are constructive—to identify what you're able to create and offer that's of some unique value to others. The instant you were conceived, a set of DNA came into being that's unique in all of human history. Construction began, so to speak, on the blueprint of a human being unique from any of the billions of human beings conceived before or since. And that

uniqueness enables *everyone* to do *something* (or multiple things!) uniquely well, so you have to figure out what that is and do it. George Washington Carver explained it spiritually: "What you are is God's gift to you; what you make of yourself is your gift to God." Adam Smith explained it economically in his 1776 classic (notably the year in which the United States was founded), *The Wealth of Nations*: "division of labor" based on the diversity of human strengths is ultimately how we, individually and collectively, fulfill our needs plus as many of our wants as possible (and as we've seen earlier in this book, it also happens to be what makes us happiest).

Talk to some Americans whom you consider to be highly successful long-term. Chances are, they didn't know about me or my prescription back when they started out, yet they've taken most if not all of the above steps, either because of how they were raised and educated or because they chose to *think* carefully and critically about their behavior despite cultural influences to the contrary. Following my Prescription for Personal Prosperity is all about owning—all about personal responsibility—and any able-bodied, able-minded individual of either gender, of any race, and from any socioeconomic background can do it (it's *free*). It won't guarantee that you'll become wealthy, but I believe that it will significantly increase your chances of having not only your needs but also many of your wants fulfilled in life. I believe it will also significantly increase your chances of achieving a sense of self-esteem justified by accomplishments born of self-efficacy, self-reliance, and self-confidence. In addition, I believe it will significantly increase your chances of actually capturing, rather than just pursuing, sustained happiness. If you haven't followed the prescription before, but you start now, I believe you can still achieve significant positive changes in your life, as I recommended to Pam Ramos.

PETITIONING THE PRESIDENT VS. PERSONAL RESPONSIBILITY

In May 2014 Pam Ramos penned an article that was published at Salon.com about her experience as a four-year Walmart store employee in Mountain View, California. The article was titled "My Personal Walmart Nightmare: You Won't Believe What Life Is Like Working There,"[38] and she wrote it in advance of a visit by the U.S. president to the store where she worked. She didn't say how old she was, but she mentioned being worried about her grandchildren's future, and based on a photograph accompanying her article, I surmised that she was in her fifties at the time. She also didn't say exactly what her job entailed, but given its part-time nature coupled with its low hourly wage, I surmised that it involved checking, stocking shelves, assisting customers on the sales floor, and so on rather than doing anything supervisory or managerial. She told readers that she was working thirty-two hours per week on average and that her take-home pay was approximately $400 every two weeks, on which she couldn't always afford to buy enough food. She also told readers that she had recently been stricken with a yet-to-be diagnosed illness, and while Walmart did provide her with health insurance, she hadn't been able to pay her rent because her insurance required copays of $30 to $100 for physicians' office visits and various diagnostic tests, so she had been forced to move in with her adult son. Ms. Ramos also lamented that she had no savings, having lived paycheck-to-paycheck for years, while Walmart was earning annual profits of $16 billion. She concluded with her proposed solution to her financial problems and those of her similarly situated coworkers. It was for President Obama to "tell Walmart to pay us enough to cover the bills and take care of our families."

Despite the apparent unskilled nature of her job, Ms. Ramos's writing indicated a level of intelligence that I surmised, were she in good physical health, would make her capable of doing more skilled work, perhaps even administrative work. She didn't mention it, but beneath the article, Salon.com printed a disclosure that she was a member of the "Organization United for Respect at Walmart" (OUR Walmart for short), which is a proxy for the United Food and Commercial Workers International Union (UFCW). I felt sorry for Ms. Ramos, especially given her health problems, which I hope have since resolved, but I saw an opportunity to compare and contrast the power of the president to solve her problems to the power of personal responsibility. I posted a link to her article on my Facebook page for my fans to read, along with this response from me, titled "Advice to Walmart employee Pam Ramos":

First off, Ms. Ramos, I'm very sorry if you're sick. There's little I can do to help you with that (other than say a prayer for you, which I will), but assuming you recover and continue working, as I hope you do, I may be able to help you with what's really holding you back in your career: your attitude.

You seem to think that it's someone's responsibility other than yours to meet your needs and wants in life. It's not. It's not your employer's responsibility; it's not your fellow Americans' responsibility; it's your responsibility. Based on the quality of your writing and the fact that you've apparently been working at Walmart for some time now, you appear to me to have been substantially intact mentally and physically in your adult life, so if you're so uneducated, so unskilled, that you can't create more than $200 per week of value for somebody else, why is that?

Your fellow Americans made a free public education available to you through high school, and they even made a college education highly accessible to you by offering to loan you the money to complete it so long as you eventually, over several decades if necessary, paid it back. Did you avail yourself of those opportunities? Did you perhaps quit school prematurely? Did you ever commit a crime? Did you ever get yourself addicted to anything? And did you ever choose to make a child out of wedlock? I recite those possibilities because they're the four fastest "bullet trains to poverty" for able-bodied/minded Americans, and while you may never have traveled on any of them, if you ever did, you took that trip voluntarily.

Now, let me help you understand Walmart's relationship with you: Walmart needs stuff done, a lot of unskilled labor apparently, which is precisely what you have to sell apparently. Walmart apparently told you how much money an hour of your unskilled labor was worth to it, you apparently accepted its offer, and you've apparently been voluntarily trading your unskilled labor for Walmart's money on that basis for some time now. That's it, then, Ms. Ramos. If you think your labor's worth more money per hour than you're getting for it, then demand more, and if Walmart won't pay what you think you deserve, then peddle your labor elsewhere (many of your fellow Americans even work more than one job!), and if nobody will pay what you think it's worth, then it's not worth that much, period. Walmart's only responsibility to you (in the money-for-labor transaction—it has ancillary legal obligations such as keeping your workplace reasonably safe) is to pay you the money that it promised to pay you for the work that you've completed, and apparently it's done that.

But that's apparently not all it has done. Apparently it has also helped you out with your healthcare expenses, even though it's not yet required by law to do so (and even if/when it is required by law to do so, it could simply keep your hours below thirty per week, every week, and avoid the requirement—believe me, it could find people who'd put in under thirty hours per week doing whatever it is that you do, just for the money, no health insurance at all). Yet, you complain that its voluntary help with your healthcare expenses isn't good enough. You want it to pay all of your healthcare expenses, even though it apparently had exactly nothing to do with causing your current health problems (which again, I'm sorry you're having).

And so what do you propose to change? Do you propose to change yourself, to perhaps go back to school and improve your skills so that you can increase your value to Walmart, or perhaps to some other employer, perhaps in some other place? No. You propose to have the President of the United States "tell" Walmart to simply hand you more money than your services are worth to it so that you can have a higher standard of living, as if that's why Walmart's in business, to make sure you're satisfied with your standard of living. It's not. It's in business to make money for its shareholders (some of which the shareholders can then, as they see fit, donate to charities which help people in dire straits, and many shareholders do so). It makes money by helping its customers to be satisfied with *their* standards of living (by saving them money on basic household items that they need and want). Therefore, it really shouldn't be paying more than the market will bear for any of its supplies, neither for the products on its shelves nor for the labor to put them there.

Walmart's apparently not your problem, Ms. Ramos. Your self-entitled attitude is, and while again, if you're ill, I hope and pray that you recover, fully and quickly, as long as you harbor that attitude, you'll likely never be satisfied with your life, no matter what the President (the same President who promised you free health care, by the way) does.

Think I wasn't compassionate enough toward Ms. Ramos? I suppose that depends on what you think is compassionate. I don't think it's compassionate to encourage or enable someone to externalize responsibility for circumstances that they've largely created or to go on moaning about that which they have the ability to change. The power of personal responsibility is far more likely to improve their lives in the long run than any president, any government program, or even any voluntarily contributed handout that requires them neither to improve themselves nor to do anything of value for others in return. I don't think it's compassionate to deprive them of that power.

PERSONALLY
RESPONSIBLE HAPPINESS

The power of personal responsibility not only can make one's behavior more constructive and make one more contented with what one has in life, it can also make a person happier. Just as a person who's accountable for destructive behavior in the past is then both empowered and obligated to behave more constructively in the future; and just as a person who's accountable for what they haven't had in the past is then both empowered and obligated to become more content with what they have in the future; so also is a person who's accountable for pursuing happiness misguidedly in the past then empowered and obligated to pursue it more meaningfully in the future.

Viktor Frankl—psychiatrist, Holocaust survivor, and author of *Man's Search for Meaning*—epitomized the power of personal responsibility in this regard: one's *choice* to seek meaning in one's life, even in the grip of profound suffering. He didn't take personal responsibility for the circumstances of his unjust imprisonment; the mass psychopathy of the Nazi regime (of which today's ISIS is frighteningly reminiscent) was solely responsible for that. But Frankl did take personal responsibility to continue to try to fulfill what he believed to be his purpose in life despite those horrific circumstances. While imprisoned in the Nazi concentration camp Theresienstadt (I've visited there; it must've been horrific), he continued to practice medicine and produced educational programs on coping skills for his fellow prisoners. He later wrote, "I grasped the meaning of the greatest secret that human poetry and human thought and belief have to impart: The salvation of man is through love and in love." In other words, he found meaning, and a modicum of peace if not happiness per se, even in the face of despair, by caring and creating something of value for others. Frankl lived to the age of ninety-two, and what may well have been the secret to his longevity has been corroborated by a study that began in the late 1930s and followed 268 male Harvard

University students throughout the remainders of their lives. The Grant Study, as it has come to be known, found that "the capacity to love and be loved was the single strength most clearly associated with subjective well-being at age eighty."[39]

When viewed in this context, it's particularly sad how many of those celebrities whom I mentioned in Chapter 1—the ones who've become suicidal despite having attained wealth, fame, and accolades—*have* cared deeply and *have* created prolifically. Apparently they haven't seen in themselves what others have seen in them, in large part, I believe, because they've pursued happiness in the wrong way. Instead of pursuing it as Viktor Frankl did—as a byproduct of caring and creating something of value for others—I believe they've often pursued it as an end, and all too often, they've found it to be literally a dead end.

In my experience, many people who acquire wealth rapidly, as many celebrities have, are surprised by how much it *can't* buy them. Accordingly, studies show that the happiest people on the planet aren't necessarily the most privileged or prosperous but rather are those with a strong sense of purpose and a belief that they're making progress toward fulfilling that purpose. This partly explains why, when I travel around the world, I find a lot of happy people in places where the standards of living come nowhere close to meeting most Americans' expectations. Whether one's unique gifts lend themselves to the entertainment of millions, or to the relatively unsung raising of children into productive, compassionate (and therefore, happy) adults, if pursued properly, I believe that happiness ultimately is attainable even for those who face profound hardships in life. *Everyone* can contribute *something* uniquely good to the human condition, and when we do that, we end up feeling happy, while the world ends up getting something it needs. The happiness that we end up feeling—in contrast to the hedonistic, nihilistic *illusion* of happiness, which so many misguided celebrities and everyday Americans have been pursuing in recent years—is a much more genuine, much longer-lasting, much more *meaningful* form of happiness.

PERSONALLY RESPONSIBLE SAFETY

Having been involved in the coverage of so many preventable crime tragedies over the years, I feel compelled to highlight the power of personal responsibility to keep you safer, too. I have tremendous respect for law enforcement officers—my dad was one—but if you ever become a victim of a crime, chances are there isn't going to be a law enforcement officer standing nearby to come to your rescue. They'll get there as fast as they can, but by the time they arrive, in most cases, damage will already have been done. Even if they catch the perpetrator(s), the justice system can administer punishment, but it can't turn back time and erase the crime. That's why we all have an obligation to take personal responsibility for our safety.

Some people don't like it when I say that. I've been in yelling matches on television when I've pointed out how missing or murdered young women might have avoided those fates, and female hosts or panelists have accused me of "blaming the victim." Of course I've never blamed a victim. In each of those cases, the perpetrators were solely responsible for the crimes, and the victims *should* have been able to leave their doors unlocked, get as intoxicated as they liked, leave bars with strangers about whom they knew virtually nothing, and so on without having to worry about their safety. But that's fantasy, not reality. In reality, evil people exist, and they'll seize any opportunity to take whatever they want—an unlocked door, an impaired victim, a victim who's overly trusting. And evil people are difficult to spot, even for those of us with a great deal of training and experience, so by the time the average person notices them, it's too often too late.

Rather than blaming the victims, I've merely tried to draw some good from the tragedies that I've analyzed by using those tragedies to illustrate principles that could save lives in the future. Until fantasy becomes reality, at the very least, we all need to take proactive steps to keep ourselves out of harm's way—for example, locking doors, going places with others whom we're confident we can trust, keeping our minds clear enough to look out for ourselves and our friends, and withholding our full trust until it's earned. And to the extent that we're able to also prepare and equip ourselves to be appropriately reactive to threats that we may nevertheless encounter—such as drawing attention to ourselves and defending ourselves at least long enough for help to arrive—we're going to be even safer.

Widely reported incidents of sexual assaults on college campuses in 2014 and 2015 illustrate the power of personal responsibility to keep one safe not only from criminal harm (by keeping oneself out of harm's way) but also from reputational harm. Based on those reports, one might've concluded that the typical American male college student is a would-be rapist when, statistically speaking, just a few are; the vast majority are not. Rapes do happen on college campuses, and when they do, the perpetrators need to be apprehended, prosecuted, and punished severely. More often, though, a male and female student, both adults, get intoxicated but remain conscious and lucid enough to make (not necessarily good) decisions about their behavior, and they have consensual sex, which one of them then regrets in the sober light of day for any number of reasons. To be sure, rape is a sociopathic behavior; however, so is false reporting of rape. Deflection of blame can do irreversible damage, not only by harming the reputations of those falsely accused, but also by casting doubt on the claims of true rape victims going forward.

Regretted sex is not rape. If one's physically forced, if one's unconscious, if one's surreptitiously intoxicated, that's rape. But if none of that happens—for example, if both participants' judgments are simply impaired by voluntary intoxication—then either they're both rapists or neither one's a rapist. Some people who call themselves feminists claim that only the male in that mutual-impaired-judgment scenario remains personally responsible for his behavior, but I think it's actually insulting to women to suggest that an intoxicated male brain continues to function at a sober adult level while a similarly intoxicated female brain takes on a childlike incapacity to consent. Avoidance of both regretted sex and allegations of sexual impropriety is a personal responsibility issue on both participants' parts. People often act first and think later. The process seems simple enough, but people often avoid it. Some things in life are out of our control, but our actions are not. Stop and think before you take that drink and jump into bed with someone. Is this what you would do if you were sober? There is no such thing as "casual sex."

PERSONALLY
RESPONSIBLE PARENTING

By leveraging the power of personal responsibility, individuals can avoid repeating past destructive behavior, behave better, be more productive and more content with what they have, be happier, and be safer from various kinds of threats in life. And when groups of individuals leverage the power of personal responsibility to achieve those results in their lives, we end up with families, organizations, and ultimately societies that are less destructive, more productive, happier, and safer. Those who built America into the freest, most prosperous society in history were what you might call "rugged individualists." That's not to say that they didn't care about one another; in fact, they were, for the most part, quite generous. They understood, though, that as part of something larger than themselves—the country—they had personal responsibilities to be all they could be, to educate themselves, to acquire and develop unique skills, to work hard, to take care of themselves and their families, to contribute something of value to their society, to be prepared to defend themselves and their families and their society if necessary, to neither seek nor accept assistance they didn't really need.

And they were wildly successful, which has had an unintended consequence, as sustained prosperity and security often do: the society that they built has grown soft in some ways. In recent years, we've been producing fewer rugged individualists and more soft collectivists; such people are more focused on self-comfort, don't necessarily see themselves as part of something larger, aren't as motivated to be all they can be, talk a lot about their rights and others' obligations, expect others to help them take care of and protect them and their families, and accept unneeded assistance as if it were owed them. How, then, do we once again leverage the power of personal responsibility at the group and, ultimately, the societal level? Here again, it starts at home.

As I've said previously, if you're a parent of a minor child, your mission in life is to get your child to the age of majority as physically, mentally, socially, morally, and spiritually healthy and as well-educated as possible. You need to equip your child with strong values upon which to build a strong foundation as an adult, enabling him or her to continue taking good care of him- or herself, and to be a positive contributor to relationships, organizations, and society. To that end, parents need to teach and model self-regulation along with other core skills and values, like respect for other people and their property, beginning very early in their children's lives. Parents are the foremost determinants of whether their children become conscientious, and that determination is critical. Dictionary.com defines "conscientious" as "governed by conscience; controlled by or done according to one's inner sense of what is right; principled," making it a chief component of personal responsibility. Writing for the *New York Times*' Motherlode blog in 2013, fellow psychologist Lisa Damour deftly summarized research findings that childhood conscientiousness is a better predictor of adult well-being—as defined by "health, relationships, and a sense of mastery in one's chosen pursuits"—than childhood happiness (affirming the misguidedness of those parents from back in Chapter 1 for whom their children's happiness is the sine qua non of their existence!).

In Chapter 5, I wrote about the need to allow kids to experience consequences, hurts, regrets, shames, and failures—within reason—because that's how they learn forward thinking, delayed gratification, resilience, perseverance, and self-reliance. Overprotected kids often don't handle freedom well when they finally get it. At the same time, underprotected (i.e., neglected) kids often don't handle personal responsibility well when they're finally expected to exercise it. It's human nature to want freedom—freedom to choose what we want to do and ultimately who we want to be in life—but in order for each of us to have a high degree of freedom, we each must exercise a high degree of personal responsibility, so as not to exercise our freedom in ways that interfere with others' exercise of theirs. If we fail to regulate our own behavior, we invite others to regulate our behavior for us, and with it our freedom. Therefore, in order for us to be optimally free adults, the best time for us to internalize the relationship between freedom and personal responsibility is as children.

To that end, something that I call the *responsibility-power continuum* comes into play. Basically, when your child is an infant, you need to be responsible for making virtually every decision affecting that child, so the child has very little power. But by age eighteen, your child will need to be responsible for making virtually every decision affecting him/herself, and he/she then will have full legal power to do so. It's a continuum, and you don't want to take the child from one end of it to the other overnight. Locking the child up in your house and home-schooling them until age eighteen wouldn't equip them very well for life in the adult world. Ideally, you need to allow decision-making power to pass from you to your child gradually over time, as the child demonstrates the responsibility that comes with the power.

Responsibility-Power Continuum

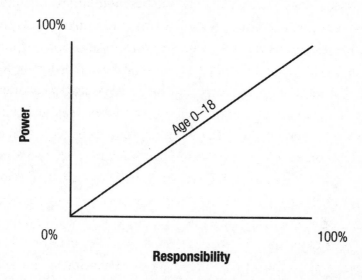

Part of allowing children to make more and more of their own decisions is allowing them to have more experiences outside of your direct supervision, and to experience the consequences thereof, throughout adolescence. For example, when I was thirteen years old, experiencing buyer's remorse after wasting a hard-earned $25 on a fad item—a Jordache belt—taught me a lot more about budgeting than if my parents had simply refused to drive me to the mall to buy it.

And no, it won't suffice to simply *tell* your child about your own learning experiences; in fact, it may not even be advisable. For instance, some so-called experts will tell you that if you used (or use) drugs, the best way to teach your kid about them is to be open and honest about your own experiences. I disagree. Yes, people can learn vicariously from the experiences of others, but in this case, that would require a fully mature mind, focused on acquiring information about what is most likely to be in its best interests in the long term. That's not the typical teenage mind. The typical teenage mind is not focused on minimizing risk, maximizing potential, or the long term; rather, it is focused on minimizing restrictions, maximizing thrills, and the short term. Therefore, as soon as you say that you smoked pot in college, even if you follow up with how stupid and dangerous you now realize it was, the typical teenage mind will process your words this way: "Dad/ Mom did it, and they're fine, so I can do it and be fine and have a conversation just like this someday with my kid." Basically, the typical teenage mind screens your words carefully for anything that can be twisted into permission or justification to do what it wants to do, and you will have just given it both. The same goes for promiscuity; you don't owe your kid the details of your sexual history. In fact, it's part of your parental mission to teach your child to recognize and respect appropriate privacy boundaries even in close relationships, such as parent-child.

Advocates of the openness-and-honesty approach will tell you that your kid will find out anyway and that she or he "will never forgive you" if you lie. First of all, I don't understand how kids, even when they become adults, are likely to find out about their parents' decades-past drug use when even major corporations' background investigators don't often uncover drug use unless it led to a conviction. Second, I'm big on the truth, but let's get real; there are times when the truth can hurt a child more than it can help, and parents are responsible for making that distinction. For example, if you're a dad and your athletically challenged fourteen-year-old asks you if you believe he can make the basketball team if he does his best at tryouts, and you believe there's no way on

Earth, do you really think he would hate you forever if he found out later that you lied when you said, "Absolutely!"? Doubt it. Same goes for perpetuating certain holiday traditions regarding the deliverers of gifts; I've never seen an adult in therapy because of "Santa Claus betrayal!" Similarly, if you're a mom, and one of your college friends lets it slip during your successful adult daughter's bachelorette party that you smoked pot in college, do you really think your daughter's going to vilify you for insisting when she was fifteen years old that you never used recreational drugs and that she shouldn't either? I doubt it.

PARENTS VS. POVERTY, PRIVILEGE, PREJUDICE, AND POLICE

Promoting conscientiousness is among the greatest gifts that parents can bestow upon children because it helps them to leverage the power of personal responsibility. As Lisa Damour encapsulated the relevant research, it portends better health, better relationships, better careers, and better overall well-being in the long term. In fact, the Longevity Project that I mentioned in Chapter 5 found conscientiousness to correlate more strongly with longevity of life than any other personality trait.[40] On the flip side, the consequences of *not* teaching personal responsibility can be tragic.

In 2014 Michael Brown, age eighteen, used marijuana, assaulted a convenience-store clerk, stole cigars, got into an altercation with a police officer, and then assaulted the officer, who shot Brown dead. Some in Ferguson and in the national media claimed it had been a senseless act driven by racism—that the officer would've acted differently had Brown been white (there was never any evidence of that). Some claimed it had been driven by "white privilege"—that somehow the officer's Caucasian race led him to feel entitled to use lethal force simply because Brown hadn't respected him (there was never any evidence presented of that either, in the officer specifically or, for that matter, in anyone, and I thought it was actually racist to even suggest it). Others claimed it had been driven by pervasive police brutality—that most police officers, including the one who shot Brown, are psychopaths who look for excuses to abuse citizens under the guise of law enforcement; a grand jury and a federal civil rights investigation determined that it was a justified act of self-defense, and I found the "brutal cop" stereotype insulting to the vast majority of officers, like my dad was, whose fine public service we often take for granted. Still others claimed it had been driven by Brown's poverty—that the broader society was somehow to blame for Brown's choices that day (it wasn't).

Shortly after the shooting, I wrote a column for WorldNet-Daily titled "Parenting—Not Poverty, Privilege, Prejudice, or Police," in which I tried to focus parents across America on how best to protect their children from ever being at the center of a crime tragedy—not by moaning about any potential sociocultural factors, over which they and their children likely would have little power anyway, but by owning their obligations to teach and model the power of personal responsibility. In that column, and in the context of the events in Ferguson, I encouraged parents to ask themselves the following five important questions:

1. *In general, have I raised the kind of person who goes through life recognizing that he or she is part of something larger than him- or herself and who therefore thinks about the impact of his or her actions upon others and tries hard not to harm anybody?* If you answer "Yes," but you've been absent from your teen's home more often than not, or if you have five different surnames residing under your roof, then I have to wonder whether you've really focused enough of your attention on your teen to have modeled this principle effectively, or whether you've instead been wrapped up in your own pursuits and have, perhaps, instilled some angry narcissism in your teen in the process.

2. *In general again, have I raised the kind of person who respects the rights of others and the law that exists to protect those rights?* If you answer "Yes," but you've been violent around your teen or been in trouble with the law yourself, then I have to wonder whether you've modeled this principle effectively.

3. Specifically now, *have I raised the kind of person who thinks it's not okay to get intoxicated illegally?* If you answer "Yes," but you've driven while intoxicated or used an illegal substance, and your teen knows about it, or if you've told your teen that it's fine with you when people violate our drug laws, then you haven't modeled this principle.

4. Specifically again, *have I raised the kind of person who'd never dream of walking into a store and stealing something?* If you answer "Yes," just consider that in a relatively recent anonymous survey of 30,000 American teens, a

third of them acknowledged having stolen something from a store within a year of taking the survey.

5. Specifically once again, *have I raised the kind of a person who, if a law enforcement officer told him or her to stop or get out of the street, he or she would comply with the officer's instruction immediately and respectfully?* If you answer "Yes," but you have modeled disrespect for law enforcement officers, then I, and more importantly you, have to wonder.

I went on to explain that if parents had answered "No" or "I don't know" to any of the above questions, their teens may be at serious risk. I suggested that parents should make an investment of substantial additional time and communication with those teens as well as an imposition of substantial additional structure and discipline in those teen's lives. I also pointed out that any parent can provide those things, whether they're black, white, rich, poor, urban, or suburban. All that's required is for the parent to have an understanding of the power of personal responsibility and to care enough about the child's long-term well-being.

PERSONALLY RESPONSIBLE PEDAGOGY

Personal responsibility starts at home, but it should continue at school. I recently came across a snippet of a University of Kansas professor discussing "incorrigible" behavior among male juveniles 100 years ago. Interestingly, he said that juvenile delinquency resulted from parental neglect, poor socialization and upbringing, innate antisocial personality traits, and in rare cases, cognitive developmental disabilities. Still sounds right to me! And then I came across the following news brief published in the *Lawrence* (KS) *Daily Journal World* (now the *Lawrence Journal World*) on February 22, 1914:

> When the members of the K.U. Girls Glee Club marched upon the platform at Fraser Hall last night for their second annual concert, they appeared as smiling and serene as usual and one could not guess the turbulence of the preceding hour. After seven o'clock last night word was received from Prof. Boynton, chairman of the eligibility committee, that three of the girls had not made their grades and could not appear in the concert. Consternation reigned supreme. The aid of Chancellor Strong was invoked, but the committee was unrelenting and at the last moment the concert was given without the leading soprano and two others, and one number could not be given at all. It was known that a few of the girls were back in their work, but the matter had been taken up with the committee some days before and it was thought that it had been arranged so they could appear for last night's program. . . . In spite of all obstacles, however, the concert was a success and the girls sang like they were inspired. The chorus numbers were good and the solos showed that K.U. possesses some splendid voices. The young ladies responded to a large number of encores and made a decided hit.

Now, I don't know how this particular kind of thing—the ineligibility of choir singers—would be handled at K.U. today, but I'm confident that at far too many American colleges and K–12 schools, similarly situated singers (or athletes) would take the

stage (or the athletic field) and sing (or play) in spite of eligibil-
ity rules because those in charge would put "sympathy" for the
irresponsible ahead of both justice for the responsible and education for all about the importance of standards and consequences.
Throughout this book, we've seen examples of well-meaning but
misguided educators doing those kinds of disservices to kids all
across America. For instance, the Los Angeles Unified School
District recently announced that, in response to mounting numbers of relatively low-level crimes committed within its schools
and to a racial disparity among the recipients of citations for such
crimes, the district's in-house police are now going to stop citing
students for a number of common offenses.

If kids aren't getting structure and discipline in their homes,
then removing it from their schools isn't going to help them. It's
just going to allow district leaders to point to reduced numbers of
offenses and pat themselves on the backs for their utterly fictitious
"success" at the kids' expense. And if in fact there's a racial disparity among the recipients of the citations, but there's a similar
racial disparity among the student body, or there's a similar racial
disparity among the students committing the offenses, then stopping the issuance of citations so that no race appears to be behaving worse than another isn't justice; it's *injustice*, to the offenders
as well as to the victims of their offenses. Moreover, if in fact
there's a disparity among the students committing the offenses,
consider this: In many parts of America, and in America overall,
there happens also to be a significant disparity when it comes
to out-of-wedlock parentage. And there's a coinciding spike in
absentee parenting, especially by fathers, who throughout human
history have played important roles as disciplinarians of kids,

especially teens. This is an example of how cultural factors can hurt our efforts to teach kids the power of personal responsibility and how public policy, like putting the concept of fault back into our divorce laws, can help us encourage personally responsible behavior (more on both of those shortly).

In an absurd confusion of correlation with causation, proponents of Los Angeles's no-punishment approach cite statistics indicating that individuals who are punished in school as minors are significantly more likely to be arrested and incarcerated as adults. Yes, they are, but that's not likely *because* they were punished in school. It's likely because the same individuals who haven't internalized conscientiousness and personal responsibility by the time they're adolescents are likely not to have internalized those things as adults. In that case, any adult who really cares about those kids' long-term well-being ought to be in favor of imposing *more* consequences for their bad behavior in school rather than fewer.

The good news is that some educators are getting it right. For instance, in September 2013 Matt Labrum, head football coach at Union High School in Roosevelt, Utah, suspended his entire team—with just days to go before the school's homecoming game, no less—after allegations that some team members had participated in an incident of cyberbullying. Labrum was quoted as having told his players that their suspensions were "not about winning games"—they were "about developing young men to go on to be fathers and be positive community members and be employable."[41] A letter distributed by Labrum and his coaching staff reportedly stated, "The lack of character we are showing off the field is outshining what we are achieving on the field. . . . We want student-athletes that are humble to learn and grow through adversity and success on and off the field." The suspended players then were given an opportunity to earn back their jerseys by following school rules, completing assigned schoolwork, performing community service, attending extra class sessions on character, and memorizing the following: "Good character is more to be praised than outstanding talent. Most talents are, to some extent, a gift. Good character, by contrast, is not given to us. We have to build it, piece by piece—by thought, by choice, courage, and determination." Ultimately, enough players earned back their jerseys for Labrum to field a team for the homecoming game. They apparently lost the game, but what they gained from Labrum's coaching is likely to be worth far more to those young men in the long run.

These same lessons hold true in the classroom—and beyond. I teach a course at the University of Kansas wherein I strive to impart to hundreds of undergraduate students psychological and legal principles to help them succeed in the American workplace, chief among those being the power of personal responsibility. Whenever I review an exam in class, for example, I tell the students who didn't do well that they have a choice of attributions for their poor performance. They can attribute it to such extrinsic factors as a bad teacher (me) or a poorly written exam (by me), in which cases they're unlikely to do anything differently and thus are highly likely to perform poorly when they take their next exams in my class as well. Alternatively, they can attribute their poor performance to such intrinsic factors as not attending my lectures (physically or mentally), not reading assignments carefully, not putting enough effort into mastering the subject matter, and yes, perhaps even a below-average capacity to master it relative to their peers, which only makes effort all the more important. If they stop moaning about that which they can't change and start owning that which they can change, then they're empowered to make positive differences in their future exam performance by taking constructive actions. Unfortunately, though it may have been the norm 100 years ago, I'm continually amazed by how many of my students seem to be hearing straight talk about personal responsibility from a teacher for the first time in my college class. We need to fix that.

Ideally, teachers' efforts should reinforce parents' efforts to promote personal responsibility and vice versa. Here in Kansas, many have been demanding for years that our state throw more money at our K–12 public schools, yet our Catholic schools consistently produce better results with substantially less funding per pupil, as national studies have also shown.[42] And that's not because Catholic schools only accept the best and brightest kids. I went to both public and Catholic schools; there were idiots and geniuses in both places, and there were good and bad teachers in both places. The big difference in results is neither money nor selectivity; it's the relationships between schools and parents. In my experience attending both types of schools and counseling students from both types of schools, it's significantly rarer for parents of kids in Catholic (and charter, and other private) schools—parents who sacrifice to pay private school tuition on top of public school property taxes—than for parents of kids in public schools to be dangerously disinterested and disengaged in their kids' academic and general development.

THE USUAL SUSPECTS

Parents need to be involved in their children's schoolwork and homework, go to parent-teacher conferences, and listen to the teachers' reports about how their children are performing and behaving at school. If teachers report disruptive behavior, parents' first "suspects" should be a discipline deficit at home, not bad teachers, and not an attention deficit (here again, most of the time, ADD more accurately describes "Adult Discipline Deficit" rather than "Attention Deficit Disorder"). Any K–12 teacher will tell you that a high percentage of students who behave in antisocial ways (destructively, disruptively, dishonestly, etc.) at school also have diagnoses of ADD (the disorder). ADD might explain inattentive, disorganized, and even rambunctious behavior (AD*H*D), but it doesn't explain antisocial behavior. In my experience, the most common explanation for kids' antisocial behavior is a lack of structure and discipline in their lives—poor parenting—and those kids' ADD diagnoses tend to mostly just be their parents' bogus externalizations of blame.

For instance, when Johnny's eighth-grade English teacher returned some graded essays to the students in her class, and Johnny didn't get one back, he told the teacher that he had turned in an essay and that she must have lost it. Though skeptical, the teacher searched high and low for an essay from Johnny and didn't find one, so she asked him if he happened to have saved a copy of the essay somewhere, like on a computer at home. Johnny said, "Yes, I'll email it to you right after school today." Two days later, Johnny brought a hard copy of the essay to the teacher, who thanked him but asked him to please still go ahead and email her a copy that evening so she could grade it at home without running the risk of "losing" it again between school and home. Well, Johnny was smart, but not smart enough. He did email the teacher a copy of his essay that evening, whereupon the teacher, one step ahead of Johnny, accessed the document's metadata (in other words, looked at its "properties") to reveal that the document had been created just one day prior, a day *after* Johnny originally had promised to email it to her and well after it had originally been due.

The next day, the teacher asked Johnny after class when, exactly, he had written the essay. Johnny lied initially, but when confronted with the metadata, he admitted that he had written it only after seeing his peers receive theirs and realizing he hadn't submitted one back when they all did. The teacher then informed Johnny that he would be receiving zero points for his essay and a referral to the principal for trying to cheat.

Now, if you're a personally responsible parent and you heard that your son had failed to do his homework and then lied about it, not once but twice, and caused all kinds of hassle for a teacher, you'd probably be furious with your son. Not Johnny's parents. They were furious with the *school*! They protested that Johnny's ADD had caused him to forget to write the essay in the first place, that he simply had panicked when he saw his peers receiving their graded essays, and that he actually *had* completed the assignment, albeit dishonestly and days after his peers were required to complete it. (And in case you're wondering, the school caved. Johnny received zero points for his essay but no discipline whatsoever for his dishonesty. Neither Johnny's parents nor the school served Johnny well in that instance. They essentially taught him that when he fails to fulfill his obligations, he might as well try lying about it.)

If parents seriously think ADD is a possibility, they should get a comprehensive diagnostic workup from a licensed psychologist. If the psychologist makes the diagnosis, the parents should ask what behavioral options can be tried before seeking medication. It's amazing how many of these "disorders" don't seem to go away with expensive medication but seem to be completely curable with a moderate, free dose of personal responsibility, administered first to the parents, then to the kids. If and when medication is deemed a necessity, parents should seek it from a child psychiatrist, not from a pediatrician or family doctor with less specialized expertise, and should follow up regularly with the psychiatrist. Parents should also continue to work on self-discipline, self-regulation, and skill-building; otherwise, the medication may just be sweeping the problem under the rug temporarily. Actually, parents may be amazed at how much behavioral progress they can make with kids simply by jointly charting the frequencies of problem behaviors and desired behaviors, challenging the kids to make the problem chart trend downward and the desired chart trend upward. Seeing a graphical representation of one's behavior and experiencing the power to alter that representation can have a significant effect on promoting personal responsibility.

PERSONALLY RESPONSIBLE ROLE MODELS

Ultimately, though, regardless of how we're parented and educated, each of us has a choice to make about how personally responsible we're going to be, and cultural factors can dramatically influence that choice. Therefore, if we could manage to swing our cultural pendulum back in the direction of personal responsibility, such that personal responsibility again became expected and even admirable, it would encourage more individuals to choose to be more responsible, which collectively would help us leverage the power of personal responsibility at the societal level. How do we even begin to do that? We can start in our own small spheres of influence by holding one another accountable and by reinforcing one another's responsible behavior. More broadly, we can stop esteeming irresponsible people just because they're good entertainers or athletes, for example, and start esteeming people who model personal responsibility.

Actor Ashton Kutcher may not be someone whose marital advice I'd endorse, but at the 2013 Teen Choice Awards, he gave some advice about personal responsibility that I not only endorse, I'm about to repeat it here. He told the mostly adolescent audience, "You can build your own life . . . so build a life. . . . Find your opportunities." He explained that an "opportunity looks a lot like hard work," reciting a list of his pre-acting jobs, which included roofing, washing dishes, and sweeping a factory floor. And while standing center-stage at an event celebrating a popular culture that all too often esteems the superficial over the meaningful, he said, "The sexiest thing in the entire world is being really smart and being thoughtful and being generous . . . . Everything else . . . it's just crap that people try to sell to you to make you feel like less. . . . Be smart, be thoughtful, and be generous." *That* was an applause-worthy performance by an actor!

In the summer of 2007 I appeared on *The O'Reilly Factor* on Fox News to discuss steroid use among professional athletes with host Bill O'Reilly. At the time, pro wrestler Chris Benoit had just murdered his entire family and then killed himself in an apparent steroid-fueled psychotic rage. Days later, poised to break the all-time Major League Baseball homerun record, Barry Bonds, though strongly implicated in a performance-enhancing drug scandal, received a standing ovation at the league's annual All-Star Game. I was disheartened to see parents alongside their kids in that audience on their feet applauding Bonds, encouraging the children to esteem a "winner" even if he was likely a cheater. So I was heartened when, in 2013, MLB commissioner Fay Vincent called for a one-strike policy—lifetime expulsions from the league for use of any banned performance-enhancing drug. *That* deserved a standing ovation from sports fans young and old! (MLB has yet to send such a strong message to its players and to America's kids about the intolerability of cheating, but at least it's being discussed.)

Although Kutcher's and Vincent's messages about personal responsibility are esteem-worthy, I wish we'd spend less time fawning over entertainers and people who do things so inherently meaningless as knocking baseballs long distances while we have soldiers and cops and surgeons saving lives every day with no fanfare. And I wish we'd spend more time heralding individuals like James Robertson and Ronald Read. In 2005, the then-forty-six-year-old Robertson's car stopped working. He couldn't afford to buy a new one, and bus routes between his Detroit home and the auto parts factory where he worked had been discontinued. So what did Robertson do? Demand that his employer pay him more or provide a company car? No. Demand that his fellow Americans support him while he looked for a different job? No. He started walking—twenty-one miles per day, round-trip, to and from the factory. Robertson did that, never missing a single day of work in that span of time, until early 2015, when a reporter for the *Detroit Free Press* discovered and told his story to the world. Since then, Robertson has received over $350,000 and a new car, thanks to an online fundraising campaign set up, not by him, but by a college student who found the story inspiring. And not surprisingly, as of this writing, Robertson's still working at the factory, every day, for $10.55 per hour. *That's* some powerful personal responsibility.

Then there's Ronald Read. Born in 1921 Read walked approximately four miles to and from school each day, becoming the first in his family to graduate from high school before joining the U.S. military. He served in World War II in North Africa, Italy, and the Pacific before returning home to Brattleboro, Vermont, in 1945, where he worked as a gas station attendant for twenty-five years and as a department store janitor for another seventeen years. His wife died in 1970, and for the remaining forty-four years of his life, he was known in his community as the friendly, frugal widower who used safety pins to hold his winter coat together and picked up scraps of wood around town to burn in his fire, and whose only indulgences included his antique Edison phonograph and his daily newspaper. So imagine the town's surprise when, upon his death in 2014 at the age of ninety-two, Read bequeathed a combined $6 million to his local library and hospital! He had quietly combined the power of education (mostly *self*-education via that daily newspaper—the *Wall Street Journal*), delayed gratification, and compound interest to make himself the single largest benefactor in history to the two community institutions he most admired. Again, *that's* some powerful personal responsibility.[43]

While it's not always easy to get one's own children, let alone an entire culture, to pay more positive attention to guys like James Robertson and Ronald Read than to guys like Barry Bonds, if a majority of us start caring enough, we can at least demand as voters that our societal *leaders* be models, and thus credible champions, of personal responsibility. For instance, if a politician's spouse can't trust him, then you can't trust him either, which makes him unfit to hold any position of esteem or authority in our society. Do you seriously think that a politician who *doesn't* mind lying to his spouse *does* mind lying to you? No, he doesn't. And the politician who'll lie to a spouse and to you is also the politician who, in the face of a blackmail threat, likely will weigh the *personal* consequences of noncompliance more heavily than the *societal* consequences of compliance.

PERSONALLY RESPONSIBLE POLICY

Once we choose personally responsible leaders, we can expect them to make public policy that promotes as much personal responsibility as possible—for example, flattening out our progressive income-tax policy so that every American who pays income tax pays the same percentage of their income. Having different rates of taxation for different strata of income allows Americans whose incomes top out in the lower strata to vote to expand government benefits for themselves and pay for those benefits by raising taxes exclusively on strata of income that they don't earn. For the 2014 income-tax year, the highest-earning 20 percent of Americans (those earning above $134,000 annually) paid 84 percent of all personal income taxes collected by the federal government. In that case, there's not much of a disincentive for most Americans to continually demand more and more from their government, which is how we became a nation whose debt is out of control. If there was no way for Americans to vote for expanded benefits for themselves by raising taxes on other Americans without raising their own taxes proportionally—that is, if we all had skin in the game—I think you'd be amazed at how many things Americans would suddenly find ways to either do without or do for themselves.

While we're asking individual citizens to be personally responsible about money by living within their means, we ought to get back to doing that as a nation. A balanced-budget amendment would be a good start. It would force us to make some tough choices about what we really need and want our government to be doing. As much as America's founders loved freedom, they still came together and formed a government. They made a social contract that imposed both taxes and behavioral restrictions upon themselves, not because they wanted the ability to meet their individual needs and wants at one another's expense, but because they understood that it actually made them *more* free. They understood that certain undertakings, like defending the nation, printing money, and building a system of roadways that connected up to one another, were best undertaken collectively. They also understood, as the Marquis de Lafayette (a French nobleman who had helped them win the war for their independence from Great Britain) said, that liberty wasn't the same thing as licentiousness.

What Lafayette meant was that, practically speaking, we're actually *less* free if we and everyone else around us can do whatever we and they please (including burglarizing a house while the owner's out working or robbing the owner at gunpoint on the street) than if there are some mutually agreed-upon restrictions to which everyone's adherence can be expected (because any violator will face the collective enforcement power of the others). The government originally was formed and given the power to tax so that it could undertake certain physical and financial infrastructural and public-safety functions essential to the operation of the nation, not to make sure that everyone in it had enough to eat and roofs over their heads. That's not to say that America's founders had no sense of duty to help those who couldn't help themselves, but they understood this duty to belong not to their *government* but to them as a *society*. It was a duty to be undertaken voluntarily, never forced upon anyone, for the following four important reasons:

1. Coercion of assistance to needy members of society obviates the givers' personal responsibility to be generous and helpful in life voluntarily; it destroys the motivation to be charitable.

2. A guarantee of assistance obviates the recipients' personal responsibility to do everything they can do for themselves; it destroys motivation to be self-reliant and productive.

3. Voluntary charity is far more efficient and effective than the government could ever be at delivering assistance to those who truly need it.

4. When we abdicate either our personal responsibility to take care of one another or our personal responsibility to take care of ourselves—let alone both!—to the

government, we necessarily also abdicate freedom. We essentially give the government a perfect pretext to impose further restrictions on our behavior. For example, when we abdicate responsibility for our healthcare bills to the government, then we really can't be surprised when the government uses that expense as its excuse to restrict what kinds of foods we can eat.

It's already happening. Some local officials are trying to place additional sales taxes on food and beverage items that they deem unhealthy. Others are trying to limit the portions of certain items, such as soft drinks, that can be sold in their jurisdictions. Still others are trying to restrict the use of certain ingredients, such as sodium, and to completely ban certain ingredients, such as trans fats. And at the federal level, proposed new labeling regulations require restaurants to publish calorie counts for every menu offering, every possible way you could order it.[44] What do you think that's going to do to the number of choices we'll be offered? We'll get fewer. And to whom do you think restaurants are going to pass on the costs of such regulations? Us. Remember, freedom and personal responsibility go hand in hand. We need to think very carefully as a society about which responsibilities are our government's and which are ours, both individually and in voluntary cooperation with one another.

But once a society forms a government—and particularly when it gives that government the power to tax its citizens—there's a huge temptation for the society to pawn off on that government a litany of societal problems that government wasn't set up and isn't well-suited to solve. For example, it may be tempting to say, "Gee, we ought to help the poor, so let's just have the government force everyone to help the poor by raising everyone's taxes and redistributing the additional revenue." It doesn't work though. Since the 1960s, the United States federal government has redistributed over $22 *trillion* (more than our entire current national debt and three times the cost of all of our wars since the Revolution!)[45] in an effort to eradicate poverty, and guess what? The poverty rate in America remains largely unchanged. So here again, we have to try something new—make that something old: personal responsibility.

If and when we decide that we want the government to fund a public assistance program, we have to make sure that it's narrowly tailored to those who are truly incapable of meeting the targeted need for themselves, and we have to make sure they're using it for that purpose. For example, in early 2015, legislators in my home state of Kansas introduced a bill to prevent public assistance dollars from being used for expenditures on nonessential goods and services, including alcoholic beverages, cigarettes, gambling, pornography, cruises, and psychic readings. Sound obvious? Well, to many Americans today, it's not. One legislator called the bill "punitive and highly judgmental," and the CEO of an advocacy group for needy children said it felt "mean-spirited." Even comedian and former host of *The Daily Show* Jon Stewart weighed in, ranting that if Kansans weren't allowed to use public assistance dollars on the banned goods and services, then the state of Kansas shouldn't be allowed to use federal highway funds to pave roads. The governor, however, injected a dose of sanity into the debate, explaining that the bill, which ultimately passed, was about incentivizing people to assume personal responsibility for fulfilling their wants in life. "It is important," he said, "that every chance we get, we encourage people to get back into the marketplace, get back into the job market."[46]

At the federal level, our recent endeavor to provide health insurance to all Americans is a good illustration of how *not* to incentivize personal responsibility via public policy. Prior, *most* Americans—the vast majority, in fact—*had* health insurance and either paid for it themselves or received it in whole or in part as a negotiated-for benefit from their employers. Yes, we still had millions of uninsured Americans, many of whom were unable to secure insurance—such as children and those with preexisting conditions—but *more* of whom were able and simply weren't inclined. So what did we do? What we always do: instead of focusing on the relatively few involuntarily uninsured and finding ways to insure them, we implemented a massively expansive, massively expensive program that covers every American, including the majority who were insured prior.

Meanwhile, in terms of reducing the costs of health care, which in turn would make health insurance more affordable, consider this. A recent three-year study[47] of over 90,000 adult employees receiving healthcare benefits from seven large companies in the United States found that more than 20 percent of those companies' employee healthcare expenditures could be attributed to the following ten risk factors:

1. High blood pressure
2. High cholesterol
3. High blood sugar
4. Depression

5. Stress
6. Obesity
7. Tobacco use
8. Poor diet
9. Lack of exercise
10. Excessive alcohol use

At least half of those factors are directly related to—if not totally reflective of—personal irresponsibility. Just think of how much money we could be saving as a nation if we focused on incentivizing personal responsibility with respect to lifestyle choices. How? By neither taking away people's personal freedom to make those choices nor sparing them personal accountability for the natural consequences thereof. To the greatest extent possible, we should allow adults' behavior to be shaped by its natural consequences. I think society's job—via public policy, in other words, the law—is just to *prevent* us from behaving in ways that are destructive to others. If we're adults and we want to behave in ways that are destructive only to ourselves and pose zero risk to anybody else, I don't think it's really any of society's business.

Take recreational drug legalization, for instance. As you know from Chapter 4, I'm not a fan of intoxication. As you also know, I'm a freedom-loving American. But knowing how personally irresponsible many individuals can be, I'm afraid to live in a country in which the vast majority of my fellow citizens experiment with recreational drugs early in life—which would happen, as it already does with alcohol, if recreational drugs were legalized. So, I won't be supporting recreational drug legalization unless and until it comes with additional public policies to ensure that individuals exercise that particular freedom in ways that don't infringe upon my exercise of other freedoms, for example, driving on public roads without having to look out for more intoxicated drivers than I already do, and that I don't have to pay the financial consequences of other people's irresponsibility. What kinds of policies am I talking about?

1. We eliminate access to any public assistance programs (e.g., Food Stamps) for anyone who tests positive for substance abuse.
2. We eliminate any mandated or taxpayer-subsidized insurance coverage of treatment for addiction.
3. We impose stiff penalties for anyone who drives stoned on our roads, gives a recreational drug to a minor, gets high with a minor in their care, etc. (I'm talking *significant* incarceration times for first offenses, and yes, I'd raise the penalties for driving drunk, too).

Think most recreational-drug legalization advocates still want legalization if it comes with policies like those? I doubt it. They seem to tend to want the freedom part without the personal responsibility part.

PERSONALLY RESPONSIBLE PUNISHMENT

Criminals are another group that likes freedom without personal responsibility. For decades now, all across America, we've been practicing catch-and-release justice, giving criminals second, third, fourth, and more chances before we finally get them off our streets for lengthy periods of time. Time and time again, when I analyze crime stories for the national media, it turns out that the perpetrators were on their fifth or sixth chances. Why have we given them so many chances to harm innocent people rather than erring on the side of public safety? Because of that misplaced "compassion" that has become all too common across America. Catch-and-release justice is *not* compassionate to victims, past and future; it's not compassionate to law enforcement officers, who end up having to risk their lives to apprehend the same criminals over and over; and it's not even compassionate to the criminals, whose behavior often escalates to the point where they either get killed or they finally do get locked up for long periods of time, but only after they've left profound, irreversible destruction and suffering in their wakes. Yet again, when it comes to deterring and preventing crime, we have to try something *old*: personal responsibility.

As I explained in Chapter 5, we're probably never going to make public policies that cause most criminals to actually care about personal responsibility, but we can make public policies that cause them to act as if they care about it. What kinds of policies? Consider the following:

1. *We can impose stiff mandatory minimum sentences* so that individual judges no longer have the discretion to perpetuate catch-and-release justice. And while that may require spending more on jails and prisons, it requires neither more taxation nor more debt. It simply requires prioritizing the protection of law-abiding citizens from attack as the first and foremost duty of government. At the global

level, that means the military, Coast Guard, and intelligence services; at the domestic level, it means law enforcement, courts, and correctional facilities.

2. *We can enact "three strikes" laws*—personally, I'd be fine with *two* strikes—mandating life, or at least multidecade, prison sentences for criminals convicted of felonies on multiple occasions (or of felonies committed after they were deported from the United States and sneaked back into the country). And, no, I generally don't care whether the final felony is something nonviolent like identity theft. How many times have you been charged with a felony? Zero, right? And how hard has it been to not commit any felonies? Easy, right? Those who commit serial felonies are telling us they have no intention of living lawfully in our society, and when they tell us that, we ought to listen and take them out of the society before they do their next damage, whatever that may be.

3. *We can eliminate concurrent sentencing,* so that judges are required to punish criminals for each and every crime of which they're convicted. It's insane that a criminal can assault a family of four with a deadly weapon, commit armed robbery of the parents, lead police on a high-speed chase, resist arrest, batter a law enforcement officer, and only serve time for a single conviction of armed robbery (because the sentences for all of the other crimes are served concurrently). That's essentially society telling criminals, "Pay us for one crime, and we'll throw in a bunch of other crimes of equal or lesser severity free."

REINFORCING RESPONSIBILITY

Finally, we can make sure that our public policies, if anything, make life easier and more rewarding—never harder and less rewarding—for people who are being personally responsible. If they're following the law, working hard, and doing well, we should essentially stay out of their hair, impose as few regulations and taxes upon them as possible, celebrate their success, and hold them up as examples of the power of personal responsibility.

CHAPTER 7

The Power of Perspective

I have but one system of ethics for men and for nations.
To be grateful, to be faithful to all engagements and
under all circumstances, to be open and generous,
promoting in the long run even the interests of both;
and I am sure it promotes their happiness.

—Thomas Jefferson

AN ENTITLEMENT VACCINE?

In Chapters 1 through 4, we saw how entitlement, in its varied
forms, is the common root of the woes about which Americans
today, individually and collectively, are moaning—unhappiness,

indebtedness, divorce, addiction, obesity, crime, and so on. Then, in Chapters 5 and 6, we saw how owning those woes instead of moaning about them—leveraging the power of personal responsibility—can act as an antidote to entitlement, transforming individuals, relationships, families, organizations, communities, and ultimately the nation for the better. Here in Chapter 7, we're going see how to inoculate oneself against entitlement by leveraging the power of a second concept without which this book wouldn't be complete: gratitude. Separately, personal responsibility and gratitude serve as formidable buffers against our current cultural bias toward entitlement, but combined, the power of personal responsibility and the power of a grateful perspective to keep us from moaning and keep us owning can't be matched.

A grateful perspective begins with the recognition that we have many good things and people in our lives, not because we're entitled to have them, but because we're blessed.

- We've been given talents and abilities that we've used to acquire things that we've needed plus many things that we've wanted—again, not because we're entitled to those talents and abilities and things but because we were blessed.
- We've been helped; in some cases we've been handed things outright by others, once again, not because we were entitled to their help or to those things, but because those people were generous.
- We've been given the opportunities to share in the lives of people who are important to us, yet again, not because we're entitled to their time and attention, but because they've loved us.

Recognizing how much we have that we're not entitled to changes our perspective on our needs and wants, our relationships, our very selves, from one of entitlement to one of profound appreciation, which serves us far better in every major facet of our lives. In our personal lives, an entitled perspective causes us to judge our worth based upon how much others are doing or sacrificing for us. A grateful perspective causes us to judge our worth based on how much of a contribution we're making to those who are important to us. And in our academic and professional lives, an entitled perspective causes us to overestimate our strengths, to underestimate our weaknesses, and to assert ourselves inappropriately. A grateful perspective causes us to evaluate ourselves honestly, to seek and accept instruction and advice from others who have greater knowledge and experience, and to take pride in exceeding others' expectations—all of which dramatically increase our chances of continuous improvement and advancement.

HALF EMPTY OR HALF FULL?

An entitled perspective focuses us on what we don't have—that proverbial half-empty glass that we resent for not being full. A grateful perspective focuses us on what we do have—the half-full glass that we appreciate for not being empty. Shifting from an entitled to a grateful perspective, then, diminishes the importance of that which one doesn't have and opens one's psyche to a humbling and genuinely fulfilling appreciation of what one does have in the here and now. Ironically, gratitude also helps us to take stock of and to patiently develop the unique talents and abilities that enable us to be of value, which is the healthy way to eventually fill the remainder of that half-full glass.

Percentage of Americans Who See the Glass Half-Empty vs. Half-Full[48]

27%

73%

And as Peter Vegso, Dadi Janki, and Kelly Johnson note in *Feeling Great: Creating a Life of Optimism, Enthusiasm, and Contentment* (HCI Books, 2015), there is a relationship between gratitude and optimism.[49] Grateful people tend to be more optimistic than entitled people,[50] and optimism reinforces two important traits of personally responsible people that have been discussed throughout this book: internal locus of control and a tendency to delay gratification. People who are both grateful for what they have today and optimistic about their futures tend to think about what *they* can do to improve their future prospects and to then actually *do* those things, even when patience and short-term sacrifice are involved.[51]

GROWING UP GRATEFUL

How do we acquire a grateful perspective in life? I'm reminded of a conversation I once had with a wealthy father who was contemplating buying a very nice car for his then-teenage son. First, the father reminisced about his own high school years, how his parents couldn't afford to buy an additional car, and how jealous he was watching his friends with cars give girls rides home from school, literally leaving him in the dust as he rode his bicycle to lawn-mowing, leaf-raking, and snow-shoveling jobs at neighbors' houses until he was finally able to buy his first, very-used, car after graduation. Some forty years later, having built a very successful business, the father then shifted gears to talk about the son, telling me, "I don't want him to have to do the things I had to do." Incredulous, I blurted out, "Why the hell not?"

Regaining my composure, I explained, "Those things you had to do helped motivate you to become the success that you are today. It wasn't acceptable to you to have to watch less-deserving people be able to do things for themselves and others that you couldn't do, so you worked hard physically, you sacrificed, you educated yourself, you worked even harder intellectually, and look at yourself now. You know what it means to be able to buy this car that you're thinking about buying for him. So *why* would you ever want to deprive him of the chance to become what you've become, to feel the pride that you feel, and to see life from the grateful perspective that you have?" (In case you're curious, he still bought the car, which the son promptly wrecked.)

Unfortunately, he and his son weren't alone. A few years later, in 2015, Bloomberg.com published an article about parents who were sacrificing their retirement savings in order to help their adult children financially. According to this article, 31 percent of parents whose adult children are part of the millennial generation, born after 1980, were supporting those adult children in some financial way.[52] It said that 13 percent were contributing to their children's rent (and according to Forbes, 45 percent of recent college graduates are living with their parents), 24 percent were helping their children make student-loan payments, 28 percent were contributing to their children's healthcare expenses, 41 percent were helping their children pay transportation expenses (car payments presumably), and 59 percent were contributing to their children's miscellaneous "other" expenses.[53]

And for the foreseeable future, those numbers appear only to be headed upward. A 2015 poll found that 65 percent of parents of high school seniors anticipate financially supporting their children for up to five years *after* they graduate from college. What's worse, that same poll found that 68 percent of high school seniors *expect* their parents' financial support after college![54] Now, before you feel sorry for these parents, remember what we've seen earlier in this book. If their adult children aren't self-sufficient, the parenting that those children received as minors probably had a lot to do with it. Recognizing that on some level, catering to their children's moaning instead of insisting that they start owning the responsibility for their own financial support may assuage some parents' guilt, but now more than ever, it's not really helping the children in the long run. It's simply enabling them not to grow up.

Nevertheless, when contemplating how long she'd continue supporting her children, one of the parents quoted in the Bloomberg.com article said, "We're between a rock and a hard place because we want our kids to be happy." Ironically, had she and the other parents described above been more careful not to breed entitlement and more committed to instead instilling gratitude in their children, not only would those parents likely have prompted greater motivation, greater productivity, better stewardship of property, and more interpersonal generosity in their children, but also, indirectly, they would much more likely have facilitated their children's long-term happiness. A grateful perspective, as we've seen time and again throughout this book, tends to start at home, with parents, but it doesn't end there. Schools and educators have important roles to play as well.

FROM GREATNESS TO GRATITUDE

I always enjoy watching the Olympics, and not because it really matters much to me whether a fellow American can run or ski faster than someone from another country. I enjoy watching the Olympics for two main reasons. First, I like watching people develop talents that they've been given to their fullest because, as you know, I believe that's half of what we're all supposed to be doing in life. And second, I like what it says about the United States. Consider this: China has over a billion people, between three and four times the population of the U.S., and it has the ability to select any of its young citizens at early ages and essentially force them to train to compete in international athletic competitions. Chinese gymnasts, for example, are selected at age three and sent to live in gymnastics training camps, seeing their families sometimes as infrequently as once a year. In theory, then, China *should* win every event, but it doesn't—not even close. Why not?

Because, for all its talent and all its coerciveness, the Chinese system is neither the most efficient nor the most effective way to get the most out of people. Of course, we have some overbearing, borderline tyrannical parents here in the U.S. who probably push their kids almost as hard as the Chinese do, but still, those parents don't get to pick kids to push. They have to take the kids they've got and try to help them make the most of what talent they have. When Team U.S.A. wins, I believe that it not only demonstrates the triumph of individuals, but it also demonstrates the triumph of the American system, in which people are free to choose which talents they wish to develop, whether they're talents that have profound life-and-death implications (like doing the best brain surgery) or talents that just entertain other people (like running or skiing fast).

Coupling historically unprecedented individual liberty with the security of the rule of law, I believe that the United States remains the *best* place on Earth to fulfill one's purpose in life, to strive to reach the fullness of one's potential, and thereby to pursue happiness. For each citizen to be able to do that requires a high degree of personal and economic freedom, and the U.S. provides both to its citizens through a democratic government with strong protections for individuals and through capitalism, which promotes competition between individuals and rewards the development of unique potential. Over the course of human history, nations that achieved power comparable to that of the United States in today's world—a lone "superpower"—typically used that power to take freedom away from people, to conquer. For most of human history, in fact, most human beings have lived in conditions in which whoever was powerful enough to kill them basically got to tell them what they could and couldn't do, that is, they haven't been free to even strive to reach the fullness of their potentials.

The United States has altered the course of human history in a positive way far more than would be expected, considering the relatively short period of that history during which the country has existed. (No, it hasn't had a perfect record, but as I noted in the Introduction to this book, it *has* literally torn itself apart and put itself back together trying to right its own wrongs.) The post–Civil War U.S. has used its power to secure more freedom for more people than ever in the history of the world, making it possible for them to create to the best of their abilities, to care to the limits of their compassion, to strive for and achieve the fullness of their potentials, to pursue, and ultimately to catch, that elusive state we call *happiness*. And we have to teach each new generation of Americans to understand and appreciate those exceptional attributes of our nation, or else we run the risk of losing them one day.

TEACHING TRADITIONS

Unfortunately, with notable exceptions, our K–12 public schools and our colleges and universities don't seem to be taking that important mission—teaching young Americans the exceptionality of America—as seriously as they once did. In fact, over the course of my lifetime, a growing percentage of American educators seem to have been ignoring, downplaying, or outright denying the importance of the values, principles, and traditions on which America was built. We supposedly no longer need marriage for optimal child-rearing. We supposedly no longer need sobriety for physically and mentally healthy citizens. We supposedly no longer need moral judgments for a healthy culture. We supposedly no longer need consequences for the deterrence of destructive behavior. We supposedly no longer need work ethic for constructive behavior. And we supposedly no longer need to teach our young people how traditions such as the above in fact made the society in which they're growing up as free and prosperous as it is.

The truth is, rarely (if ever) in all of human history has a tradition that helped a society be successful for hundreds of years all of a sudden become unnecessary. If we're going to remain the freest, most prosperous nation in human history, we need all of the above. A grave danger for successful societies is the pervasive assumption that they can abandon the traditions that made them successful yet remain successful. Rome couldn't, and neither can America. But this illustrates the problem: Many young Americans today don't *know* what happened to Rome. Colleges and universities across America are eliminating Western civilization course requirements, making it possible for one to have an American college degree hanging on one's wall and yet to know nothing about how the economic and governmental systems of the nation in which it was earned came to be. So parents, along with K–12 public and private educators who understand how critical this is, must recommit themselves to teaching kids about American history and government and about how it is that this nation has given them so much for which to be grateful.

GRATITUDE GOES GLOBAL

Thanksgiving is my favorite holiday, not because of the food, and not because of the football, but because it's all about gratitude—no presents, no cards, not really even any decorations (not that I'm against any of that), just gratitude. The food that we share on Thanksgiving has its traditional roots in a celebration of gratitude for the survival of our nation's founding community, and as I enjoy it each year, I'm reminded to be grateful for all that has been achieved in and by this nation since then. A lot of moaning goes on here, some of it justified, much of it unjustified, and most of it not very constructive (i.e., not doing much to improve the country or the lives of the moaners). I've been fortunate enough to travel around the world relatively early in life (thirty-five countries so far and seven continents), and those experiences have really put our nation's blessings in perspective for me.

At any given moment, most of us who live here go about our daily activities without giving a thought to the possibility of the country being attacked. That's because hundreds of thousands of people willingly enlisted—some for service here, the rest spread throughout the world in a wide variety of inhospitable conditions—and spend all day, every day, thinking about it. I've been places where that kind of national security hasn't existed in any living citizen's lifetime. Almost every one of us who lives here can pick up a telephone at any moment, press three little buttons, and expect that, within minutes, trained professionals will arrive on the scene to protect us and our property from crime, health crises, natural disasters—just about any emergency situation that could arise. I've been places where that kind of societal concern for individuals is a completely foreign concept.

Virtually all of us can turn a handle and watch clean, drinkable water come pouring forth, flip a switch and watch darkness become light, open a door and pull out a cold drink or well-preserved food, make our environments warmer or cooler with a simple touch, and have instant access to more entertainment and information than we could possibly take in at the touch of a button, twenty-four hours a day, seven days a week. I've been to places where that kind of reliable convenience would seem like something out of a futuristic television show (if there were televisions in virtually every home like there are here).

The vast majority of us have the choice of getting into either our own vehicles or cheap, clean public transportation and traveling just minutes to huge indoor markets, filled with thousands of foods from all over the world (usually multiple kinds of each) and virtually everything else we need for daily living. I've been places where the "supermarkets" were smaller than what we call "convenience stores," where people's floors were dirt, where electricity may or may not have been available (certainly not reliably), and traveling even a few miles was a dangerous ordeal.

And believe it or not, most of the people I've met and observed in those places have seemed happy. Apparently, they've had grateful perspectives on life. They apparently weren't comparing what they had to what anyone else had, and if they had the basic necessities of life, they apparently felt blessed. In America, especially lately, we hear a lot about people's wages not being high enough, health care not being cheap enough, credit not being loose enough, gas prices not being low enough, the stock market not recovering fast enough, and on and on and on.

POVERTY PERSPECTIVE

I was floored in 2013 when President Barack Obama even went so far as to say that, of anywhere in the world, "inequality is most pronounced in our country"! Now I know that the president has been to third-world regions, as I have, so I don't know how he could've missed the vastness of the wealth disparities there. Sadly, there are places in this world where kids, substituting for parents who've been killed in violent clashes or who've died of epidemics like AIDS, struggle to keep their younger siblings from starving, literally living in garbage dumps. Now *that's* poverty, and it's often attributable to violent oppression, pervasive corruption, and an accompanying lack of opportunity for upward socioeconomic mobility.

Contrast that to the United States, where, according to the Census Bureau, even among households with poverty-level incomes,

- Ninety-seven percent have both stoves and refrigerators.
- Ninety-six percent have televisions—with 83 percent also having video recording/playback devices, nearly 65 percent having cable or satellite programming, and over 50 percent having video gaming systems.
- Ninety-three percent have microwave ovens.
- Eight-six percent have air conditioners.
- Eighty percent have mobile phones.
- Nearly 75 percent have at least one automobile.

- Over 65 percent have washers and dryers.
- Fifty-eight percent have computers.
- Access to health care is widespread—with access to *emergency* health care being near universal.

In the United States, where we uphold the rule of law, the wealth disparities that exist more often are attributable to people's choices rather than to a lack of opportunity. Of course, we have some people in extreme need here, but in general, on balance, even America's truly needy (which our loudest moaners usually are not) are relatively advantaged by global comparison. On top of that, each and every one of us has the right to moan as much and as indignantly as we like about the way things are here with zero fear of being silenced by the government for the views we express. We also get to be thankful to whomever or whatever we believe in, or to believe in nothing, with zero fear of being penalized for the beliefs that we hold. I wish that everyone reading this book would have a chance to travel around the world, to compare what exists elsewhere to what exists here in the United States, and to gain that firsthand perspective on how much we have to be grateful for.

A GRATITUDE PRESCRIPTION

In the meantime, closer to home, as we've seen throughout this book, regardless of the parenting we received (or didn't receive), regardless of the education we received (or didn't receive), when it comes to our perspective on life—entitled or grateful—each of us ultimately has a choice. We each can choose to expand our awareness beyond ourselves and to be grateful for the many ways in which we're relatively advantaged rather than dwelling on what we perceive as our disadvantages. We can choose to spend less time with the media (both social and—I hope I don't get fired for saying this—television), to spend less time with the mirror, and to spend more time with each other, especially looking out for each other. And we can choose to value people over things and to keep our expectations proportional to our contributions, both economically and interpersonally.

In Chapter 6, I gave an eight-step prescription for anyone who wants to prosper in America. Now, here's my four-step prescription for anyone who wants to choose a more grateful perspective on life:

1. **Get your priorities straight.** You first must differentiate between needs and wants and then focus on fulfilling needs *before* wants. There's a tremendous sense of relief that comes from realizing how many of the things you've been chasing in life are things you don't really need. It also means putting *people* first, recognizing that other people's time and attention and love mean far more in life than things and that our greatest, truest happiness comes not from things but from being meaningful to others. I said it in my prosperity prescription, but it applies here, too: Our attachments to things should be extremely loose compared to our attachments to those we love and care about. As Carl Jung observed, "The least of things with a meaning is worth more in life than the greatest of things without it."

I once heard a story about a professor who brought a
glass jar to his class, set it on a table in front of his students, placed several rocks into the jar, and then asked
the students whether the jar was full. When a student
answered, "Yes," the professor dumped a handful of
pebbles into the jar, shook the jar so that the pebbles
settled into the spaces between the rocks, and again asked
the students whether the jar was full. When another
student answered, "Yes," the professor dumped enough
sand into the jar to fill the cracks and crevices that had
remained visible between the rocks and pebbles, and again
asked the students whether the jar was full. Met with
silence this time, the professor then poured water into the
jar until it began to overflow, declared that it was then
full, and asked the students what they thought the demon-
stration was intended to illustrate. When a bright student
guessed that it was intended to illustrate how we can fit
more things into our lives if we're organized, the professor
explained that, no, it actually was intended to illustrate
how, if we put the small things into our lives first, the big
things won't fit. I don't know where that story originated
or whether it's even true, but I like it because we all have
to figure out what our "rocks" are and be sure to fit them
into our lives first. What are your rocks?

2. **Count your blessings.** You need to stop, look around, take
   inventory, and be conscious of how blessed you truly are
   if you don't have to worry about whether you're going
   to be able to feed yourself today or where you're going
   to sleep tonight. Some people like to write down their

blessings. Others like to go around the family dinner table and have each family member say something for which they're grateful. Whatever works for you, as you become more conscious of how many of your needs in life are fulfilled, you'll become more conscious also of how truly blessed you are if you have things that you *don't* need but that make your life easier or more enjoyable.

It's easy for any of us to fixate on small things that we don't have while taking for granted big things that we do have. I'm certainly guilty on this count. When I'm in a hurry to go somewhere, and I'm getting stopped at red light after red light, I tend to become highly annoyed. In those moments, I used to try to remember to think about people who were simultaneously, for example, receiving devastating diagnoses from their doctors. That effort succeeded in adding a dose of guilt to my annoyance, as I recognized how happy others would be to trade their big problems for my little one, but it didn't necessarily erase the annoyance. What I do now in those situations is to try to remember how incredibly blessed I am that I can be annoyed by something so trivial as being delayed in traffic, and for me, that gratitude erases the annoyance better than guilt did. So, I've found that even annoyances can be reframed as blessings. What blessings have you perhaps not counted lately?

3. **Give thanks.** Take time out to make regular and sincere expressions of gratitude to those who have helped meet your needs or wants in life. Let them know that you recognize that they had choices about what to do with the time or resources that they spent on you and that you

appreciate that they chose you. Studies have shown that *expressing* gratitude has observable effects on the neurochemistry of our brains and tends to make us feel less negative, less envious, less resentful, more positive, more invigorated, and more connected.

Some people like to communicate their appreciation face-to-face, and while I certainly try to do that, too, I think there's still something special about communicating it in writing. Timely, thoughtful, handwritten thank-you notes convey to others not only what you appreciate but also why you appreciate it and that you appreciate it enough to take the time to communicate your appreciation in that particular way, when you could've more easily communicated it via an email or text message. Expressing gratitude also reinforces others' generosity (see Step 4), and better late than never. Who may be overdue for an expression of appreciation from you?

4. **Be generous.** Do kind things, both for people who've done kind things for you, and, following their examples, for others you encounter. As we've seen earlier in this book *happiness*, as commonly defined by many, is often misguidedly predicated upon how much one is *getting*, while *meaning*, of which true happiness is a byproduct, is predicated upon how much one is *giving*. And just as giving thanks has been shown to enhance our mental health, studies have shown that finding meaning in our lives enhances even our physical health, making us more resistant to illnesses and more resilient when we do experience illnesses and other adversities in life.

We need not go through life, individually or collectively, indiscriminately handing out tangible gifts to
others. Tangible generosity can be a very good thing, but
whenever we give gifts with the intent of *assisting*, rather
than merely *pleasing*, the recipients, we should strive to
individualize that assistance, monitor how it's being used,
and withhold it if and when it stops assisting and starts
enabling a recipient to stagnate or regress in life. A true
gift is given with no expectation of receiving any value in
return, and considering the relatively small percentage of
adults in our society who are truly incapable of sustaining
themselves, there should be no need for a high percentage of transactions within the society to involve gifts of
value to adults for no value in return. "Giving," as I'm
using that term here, includes the value that we contribute
to our society when we develop our talents, skills, and
abilities as best we can and exchange our services and
creations with others, value for value. And generosity can
include intangibles as simple as giving a spouse or child
the benefit of the doubt and letting them off the hook for
a minor, isolated act or omission that annoys you. What
do you do, or can you do to be generous?

Following this prescription will remind you not only that you
aren't entitled but also that you're blessed, probably richly, and
remembering both of these truths will serve you well individually
and the nation well collectively. In addition, like the prescription
that I gave in Chapter 6, anyone from any background can follow this prescription starting today. And the earlier one starts

following it, the more likely one is to internalize it, to incorporate it into one's daily life, and to benefit as much as possible from it. If you're a parent of a minor child, I urge you to teach and model these lessons to and for your children. Studies show that when kids' expressions of gratitude are encouraged and reinforced, they do better in school, are less likely to be depressed, and are more likely both to internalize and to independently manifest grateful perspectives. In addition, the children's cooperation and collaboration skills, their optimism and perseverance, and their perceptions of meaning in their lives (the precursor of happiness!) all tend to increase.

TREATING CPD

America's cultural drift toward narcissistic entitlement, which I recounted earlier in this book, could be described in clinical psychological terms as a cultural personality disorder *(CPD)* with destructive ramifications at the individual, couple, family, organizational, and societal levels. But the good news is that I think our CPD is curable. I believe it is, indeed, possible to have a greater sense of meaning in our lives, better relationships, better careers, better communities, and a better country. To successfully treat our CPD we must:

• Keep in mind that each of us is part of something larger than ourselves, and that we have a duty not only to avoid doing damage to that something larger but also to contribute unique value to it.

- Strive to maintain a grateful perspective on the importance of people relative to things and on the reasonableness of our expectations of others relative to our contributions to others, both economically and interpersonally.
- Take personal responsibility for doing the right things, which requires making judgments about our own and others' behavior—in short, stop moaning and start owning!

HOPE FOR THE FUTURE

And there *is* reason to be optimistic. Just when I thought that the likes of Lindsay Lohan, Barry Bonds, and Chris Brown had won the hearts, if not the minds, of America's youth, a poll conducted by the Associated Press and MTV[55] asked 1,280 Americans between the ages of thirteen and twenty-four to list their "heroes," and the results were surprisingly encouraging. Nearly half included one or both of their parents (29 percent listed their mothers, 21 percent listed their fathers, and 16 percent listed both parents). Eleven percent included friends, 10 percent included God, 8 percent included a grandparent, 7 percent included a sibling, and 5 percent included a teacher. Some included historical figures (4 percent listed Martin Luther King Jr.), and 1 percent listed top political leaders at the time. Unspecified soldiers, firefighters, and police officers were listed frequently. But here's the really encouraging part: no celebrity, athlete, or performer was listed by more than 1 percent of respondents. Two percent of respondents did list themselves, so there are some up-and-coming narcissists out there, but not as many as might have been expected.

This survey inspired me to take a similar poll of the students in the college course that I teach, and the results were similarly encouraging. I asked my students what they were thankful for, and the most popular response was a person or persons, not things or even opportunities, with health being the second most popular response. At least these particular young Americans seem to get it. They're blessed, and so am I—and so are you.

The bottom line is that people who find themselves stuck in a moaning phase of life can begin to change—to break cycles of self-pity, entitlement, and the externalization of responsibility—*today* by finding ways to be of value to others. Whatever we may be moaning about, most of us have more ability than we may ever have thought to add value to the world, to attain the things we really need (and more), to become the people we really want to be, and to make ourselves happy in life, all by gratefully leveraging the power of personal responsibility.

Now that you've finished this book, will you leverage that power and start owning more of your destiny? Will you encourage others to leverage that power and start owning more of their destinies? By doing these things, will you play your important part in helping your community and our nation collectively to stop moaning and start owning? I hope so.

Appendix: The Russell Responsibility Rating

How much moaning (externalizing responsibility) vs. owning (internalizing responsibility) have *you* been doing? Take this brief self-scoring test to find out.

RUSSELL RESPONSIBILITY RATING

First, **take the test!**

On a scale of 1–5, 1 being lowest and 5 being highest, rate how strongly you agree with the following twenty statements. Be completely honest with yourself. Otherwise, even if you like your results, they may not mean anything.

1	2	3	4	5
Strongly Disagree				Strongly Agree

1. I prefer to make my own decisions rather than to have decisions made for me. _____

2. I should be allowed to take risks with my physical health, such as eating junk food or smoking cigarettes, if I choose to. _____

3. I prefer that rules and regulations be kept to the minimums necessary to maintain order and safety. _____

4. I should be allowed to take risks with my physical safety, such as riding a bicycle without a helmet, as long as I'm the only one who's endangered. _____

5. I'd rather have the possibility of both major successes and major failures than be guaranteed something in between. _____

6. I should be the one to decide how I help people in need rather than having my earnings taxed and redistributed for that purpose. _____

7. I value my privacy very highly and believe that my health, financial, and telecommunication records are nobody's business but mine. _____

8. I should be allowed to homeschool my child(ren) if I believe that would be a better option than the available schools. _____

9. I don't like the idea of putting extra taxes on sales of products such as soft drinks to discourage people from consuming those products. _____

10. I should be able to own a firearm to defend myself and my family if I want to. _____

11. When I've failed at things in the past, the blame for those failures has largely been mine. _____

12. It's fair that others who have made different choices than I have are doing better than I am in life. _____

13. I generally have a lot of control over how things go in my life. _____

14. Few of my problems have been caused by others or by the unfairness of life. _____

15. When I've made a mistake and caused a problem for someone close to me, I've felt very bad about it. _____

16. I try very hard not to be a burden on anyone else. _____

17. Whenever I've owed someone money, I've always paid the money back. _____

18. I'll typically wait and work hard for something I really want rather than settle for something less that I can get quicker and more easily. _____

19. I think in advance about the impact of my actions on others, and I avoid actions that others may find hurtful or offensive. _____

20. If I make a commitment, I always keep it. _____

Stop! Before you continue, have you been completely honest with yourself in your responses? If not, you may want to go back and make some adjustments. Otherwise, you may be fooling yourself when you calculate your scores.

Get your scores!

First, add up your responses to statements 1–10.

1. _____   6. _____
2. _____   7. _____
3. _____   8. _____
4. _____   9. _____
5. _____   10. _____

This is your Freedom score: _____

Next, add up your responses to statements 11–20.

11. _____   16. _____
12. _____   17. _____
13. _____   18. _____
14. _____   19. _____
15. _____   20. _____

This is your Responsibility score: _____

Plot your scores!

Plot your **Freedom** score on the horizontal axis of the matrix on the next page.

Plot your **Responsibility** score on the vertical axis of the matrix.

Finally, plot the point 90 degrees straight up from your Freedom score and 90 degrees straight to the right of your Responsibility score on the matrix on the next page (for example, if your Freedom score was 50 and your Responsibility score was also 50, then your point would be in the upper right-hand corner of the matrix). This is your *Personal Responsibility Point* (PRP).

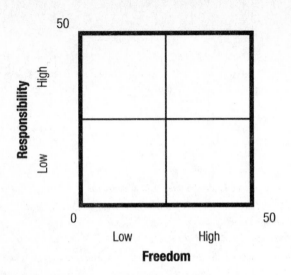

Interpret your scores!

Your Freedom score suggests how highly you value individual liberty in life.

Your Responsibility score suggests how much responsibility you take for your behaviors and outcomes in life.

If your (PRP) falls in the *lower left quadrant* of the matrix, then you may be willing to give up a significant degree of individual liberty in order to be less accountable for your behavior and to have your wants and needs met by others. While this quadrant may feel safe to some people, it can be difficult for them to maximize their potential from here.

If your (PRP) falls in the *upper left quadrant* of the matrix, then you may have a strong sense of duty toward others, and you may also have a self-sacrificing tendency. While this quadrant may feel righteous to some people, it can be challenging for them to maximize their potential from here, too, if they become overly submissive to others.

If your (PRP) falls in the *lower right quadrant* of the matrix, then you may have a sense of entitlement to do what you want to do in life while avoiding accountability for choices and expecting others to meet your wants and needs. While this quadrant may hold short-term gratification for some people, it is often quite difficult for them to maximize their potential from here.

If your (PRP) falls in the *upper right quadrant* of the matrix, then you may be in the best position from which to maximize your potential in life. America's founders wanted individual Americans to have a lot of personal freedom, but they understood that those individuals would also have to exercise a lot of personal responsibility.

Please keep in mind that if you weren't completely honest, your PRP may not accurately represent you. Consider asking an honest person who knows you well to complete the test with you in mind, and see whether your results agree.

Notes

1   *http://www.brainyquote.com/quotes/authors/s/sid_vicious.htm*

2   *http://www.foxnews.com/us/2013/08/20/library-director-says-year-old-should-step-aside-to-let-others-win-reading/*

3   *http://www.tandfonline.com/doi/pdf/10.1080/00220973.2012.745469*

4   *http://www.brookings.edu/research/reports/2014/03/18-brown-center-report-loveless.*

5   *http://www.foxnews.com/us/2013/10/22/parent-accuses-texas-high-school-football-coach-bullying-after-1-0-blowout-game/.*

6   Laura Bauer, "After College Grads Face a Nightmarish Job Market," *Kansas City Star*, December 14, 2008.

7   *http://www.heri.ucla.edu/tfsPublications.php*

8   *http://www.harpersbazaar.co.uk/fashion/fashion-news/kate-winslet-march-issue-cover*; *http://www.independent.co.uk/news/people/news/kate-winslet-says-divorce-can-be-good-for-children-because-it-helps-teach-them-how-to-struggle-10017006.html*

9   *http://hotair.com/archives/2014/02/05/pelosi-fighting-job-lock-lets-americans-follow-their-passion-like-leaving-the-workforce/*

10 Walter Mischel, *The Marshmallow Test: Mastering Self-Control* (New York: Little Brown and Company, 2014).

11 *http://dunedinstudy.otago.ac.nz/*

12 *http://www.nytimes.com/2015/06/07/opinion/sunday/why-i-defaulted-on-my-student-loans.html?_r=1*

13 *http://www.harpercollinsspeakersbureau.com/speaker/lee-siegel/*

14 *http://www.msn.com/en-us/news/other/bookkeeper-stole-dollar13m-claiming-he-was-due-for-raise/ar-AAbLjdp?ocid=iehp.*

15 *https://charactercounts.org/programs/reportcard/2008/index.html*

16 *http://www.cell.com/cell/abstract/S0092-8674-14-00611-4*

17 *http://www.abstractsonline.com/Plan/ViewAbstract.aspx?mID=3042&sKey=6dd24f14-0c48-410d-b70c-d469222d1344&cKey=cb6e99c5-1aab-4df2-8668-604d9881eaf7&mKey={2D4AF5D2-D76A-442C-A7E1-1D1A97D0251D; http://www.physiciansweekly.com/weight-loss-financial-incentives/*

18 *http://www.ncbi.nlm.nih.gov/pmc/articles/PMC3832462/*

19 *http://www.pnas.org/content/112/12/3659.abstract*

20 See Walter Mischel, "Preference for Delayed Reinforcement: An Experimental Study of a Cultural Observation," *Journal of Abnormal and Social Psychology* 56, no. 1 (January 1958): 57–61.

21 *http://www.cdc.gov/healthyyouth/obesity/facts.htm*

22 *http://www.aceshowbiz.com/news/view/00070738.html*

23 *http://www.cdc.gov/ncbddd/adhd/data.html; http://www.psychiatrictimes.com/adhd/prob lems-overdiagnosis-and-overprescribing-adhd/page/0/01*

24 *https://www.psychologytoday.com/blog/suffer-the-children/201203/why-french-kids-dont -have-adhd; http://ww2.health.wa.gov.au/~/media/Files/Corporate/general%20documents /medicines%20and%20poisons/PDF/Attentional_problems_in_children_Mgmt%20of %20ADHD.ashx*

25 "Coming Full Circle on Addiction in the Courtroom," *Journal of the Kansas Bar Associa-tion* 83, no. 5 (May 2014): 20–21.

26 *www.nhtsa.gov/staticfiles/nti/pdf/811991-DWI_Recidivism_in_USA-tsf-rn.pdf*

27 *http://www.bjs.gov/content/pub/pdf/fdluc09.pdf*

28 Lars Schulze, Isabel Dziobek, et al., "Gray Matter Abnormalities in Patients with Narcis-sistic Personality Disorder," *Journal of Psychiatric Research* 47, no. 19 (October 2013): 1363–69; DOI:10.1016/j.jpsychires.2013.05.017.

29 *http://www.huffingtonpost.com/linda-tirado/why-poor-peoples-bad-decisions-make-perfect -sense_b_4326233.html?ncid=fcbklnkushpmg00000013*

30 *http://www.familyfacts.org/briefs/42/parents-influence-on-adolescents-sexual-behavior; http://www.heritage.org/research/reports/2008/10/teen-sex-the-parent-factor*

31 Howard S. Friedman and Leslie R. Martin, *The Longevity Project: Surprising Discoveries for Health and Long Life from the Landmark Eight-Decade Study* (New York: Hudson Street Press, 2011).

32 C. B. Rose, K. Manktelow, et. al. "Psychological Factors Affecting Flood Coping Strate-gies." In *Flood Risk Assessment and management*, S. Mambretti, ed. (Billerica, MA: WIT Press, 2012).

33 *http://www.heritage.org/home/research/reports/2012/01/extended-unemployment -insurance-benefits; http://www.downsizinggovernment.org/labor/failures-of-unemployment-insurance#5; http://blogs.lse.ac.uk/europpblog/2013/08/19/setting-time-limits-on-unemploy ment-benefits-make-the-long-term-unemployed-five-times-more-likely-to-find-jobs/*

34 *http://m.ljworld.com/news/2014/jun/21/pill-burglar-discovered-dillons-ceiling-released-p/*

35 *http://www.thirteen.org/closetohome/science/html/relapse.html.*

36 For a comprehensive look about the history of the disease model of addiction, I encour-age you to read an excellent book on the subject: Gene M. Heyman, *Addiction: A Dis-order of Choice* (Cambridge, MA: Harvard University Press, 2009).

37 *http://richhabits.net/will-your-child-be-rich-or-poor/.*

38 *http://www.salon.com/2014/05/08/my_personal_wal_mart_nightmare_you_wont_believe_ what_life_is_like_working_there/*

39 George E. Vaillant, *Triumphs of Experience: The Men of the Harvard Grant Study* (Cambridge, MA: Harvard University Press, 2012).

40 Howard S. Friedman and Leslie R. Martin, *The Longevity Project: Surprising Discoveries for Health and Long Life from the Landmark Eight-Decade Study* (New York: Hudson Street Press, 2011).

41 *http://www.foxnews.com/us/2013/09/27/utah-high-school-suspended-over-character-issues-to-play-in-homecoming-game/*

42 *http://nces.ed.gov/nationsreportcard/pubs/studies/2006461.asp*

43 *http://www.reformer.com/news/ci_27453003/local-man-leaves-millions*

44 *http://www.foxnews.com/opinion/2014/01/03/top-ten-biggest-threats-to-food-freedom-in-2014.html*

45 *http://www.heritage.org/research/reports/2014/09/the-war-on-poverty-after-50-years*

46 *http://www2.ljworld.com/news/2015/apr/16/new-kansas-law-would-limit-spending-welfare-benefi*; *http://www2.ljworld.com/news/2015/apr/03/kansas-set-prevent-poor-using-aid-swimming-pools-p/*

47 *http://www.apaexcellence.org/resources/goodcompany/newsletter/article/393?__utma*

48 *http://www.deseretnews.com/article/765630382/Optimism-and-American-Dream-surviving-pragmatism-survey-shows.html?pg=all*

49 Peter Vegso, Dadi Janki, and Kelly Johnson. *Feeling Great: Creating a Life of Optimism, Enthusiasm and Contentment.* Deerfield Beach, FL: Health Communications, 2015.

50 *http://www.pursuit-of-happiness.org/science-of-happiness/positive-thinking/*

51 *http://www.athleticinsight.com/Vol8Iss2/Superstition.htm*

52 *http://www.bloomberg.com/news/articles/2015-03-05/parents-risk-retirement-to-support-millennial-kids*

53 *http://www.forbes.com/sites/kateashford/2015/05/20/post-grad-support/*

54 *http://news.salliemae.com/press-release/featured/teenagers-and-parents-agreement-when-it-comes-preparing-college-answer-resoun*

55 *http://www.mtv.com/thinkmtv/about/pdfs/APMTV_happinesspoll.pdf*

About the Author

TV's **Dr. Brian Russell** is a clinical psychologist as well as an attorney, and he also has an MBA. Among the major media psychologists, he has an incomparably well-rounded perspective on what inhibits productive behavior and facilitates destructive behavior at the individual, family, organizational, and societal levels in America. While there are many factors, he has identified two common themes among them: a pervading sense of entitlement and a diminishing sense of personal responsibility. Dr. Brian has spent countless hours treating adult and child clinical and relational problems as a psychologist, representing both high- and low-profile clients as a lawyer, and explaining the root causes of destructive behavior as an expert in courtrooms, classrooms, boardrooms, and living rooms via radio and TV. He also has traveled the world studying the commonalities that differentiate successful from unsuccessful lives, marriages, families, careers, organizations, and communities across cultures. Dr. Brian is co-host of the hit series *Fatal Vows* on the Investigation Discovery network.